GW00656489

THE *Capitol* of VIRGINIA

A LANDMARK OF AMERICAN ARCHITECTURE

For James Yorke,
with sincerest thanks,
F. Carey Howlett
June, 2003

THE *Capitol* of VIRGINIA

A LANDMARK OF AMERICAN ARCHITECTURE

FISKE KIMBALL

Revised and Expanded
from the 1989 Edition
Edited by Jon Kukla
Assisted by Martha Vick and
Sarah Shields Driggs

With a New Introduction
by Charles Brownell and
an Essay on the Capitol Model
by F. Carey Howlett

LIBRARY OF VIRGINIA

RICHMOND ▪ 2002

Published by Authority of The Library Board

Library of Congress Control Number: 2002110170

Standard Book Number: 0-88490-203-X casebound

Library of Virginia, Richmond, Virginia
© 2002 by The Library of Virginia
All rights reserved. Revised and expanded edition 2002.
Printed in the United States of America.

This book is printed on acid-free paper meeting requirements of the American Standard for Permanence of Paper for Printed Library Materials.

An earlier version of F. Carey Howlett's essay "Revealing Jefferson's Model for the Capitol of Virginia" appeared as "Thomas Jefferson's Model for the Capitol of Virginia: A New Understanding" in *Virginia Cavalcade* 51 (winter 2002): 4–15. Used by permission.

FUNDING FOR THIS PUBLICATION WAS GENEROUSLY PROVIDED BY THE CENTER FOR PALLADIAN STUDIES IN AMERICA; W. BRUCE WINGO, IN MEMORY OF HIS MOTHER, MRS. WILLIAM B. WINGO; NORFOLK SOUTHERN FOUNDATION; AND THE LIBRARY OF VIRGINIA FOUNDATION.

Contents

List of Illustrations *for* The Capitol of Virginia

Illustrations are numbered consecutively through the book.

Foreword to the 2002 Edition

The Center for Palladian Studies in America is pleased to support the publication of a new edition of Fiske Kimball's 1915 study of Jefferson and the Virginia State Capitol. Fiske Kimball, as one of the great architectural historians of the twentieth century, was devoted to the classical tradition and he opened up avenue after avenue for the study of Palladianism in the United States and abroad, beginning with Palladio's greatest American admirer, Thomas Jefferson. Kimball's study of the Virginia State Capitol stands right at the beginning of a long line of scholarship—work by Kimball himself, by historians whom he inspired, and by historians who reacted against his ideas.

The publication of a new edition of Kimball's study has been prompted by the conservation of the plaster model of the Capitol that Jefferson sent from Paris. It is incredible that this eighteenth-century model has been preserved. It provides the link based on a Roman building and the first public building in America in the temple style. F. Carey Howlett directed this brilliantly realized undertaking at the Colonial Williamsburg Foundation.

Scholarship has to be renewed for every generation. We have had to lay aside much of what Kimball said, and Charles Brownell is our guide to how ideas have changed in recent years. Nonetheless, the study of Jefferson's architecture still stands on foundations that Kimball laid, and Kimball's standards for scholarship continue to shine inspiringly.

EDMUND A. RENNOLDS, JR., PRESIDENT
CENTER FOR PALLADIAN STUDIES
IN AMERICA

fig. 1 Virginia State Capitol, 2001

Preface to the 2002 Edition

In 1989 the Library of Virginia published *The Capitol of Virginia* as a new edition of Fiske Kimball's seminal article "Thomas Jefferson and the First Monument of the Classical Revival in America." In this article, published originally in the *Journal of the American Institute of Architects* in 1915 and taken from his Ph.D. dissertation, Kimball firmly established Thomas Jefferson as the designer of the Virginia State Capitol. The 1989 publication commemorated the bicentennial of Jefferson's Capitol by complementing Kimball's text with a brief history of the State Capitol to the mid-1960s.

Two events compelled the Library to issue the current volume. The popularity of the 1989 publication and the subsequent dwindling number of copies in stock raised the question of reissuing *The Capitol of Virginia* to meet the continuing demand. The other compelling event was the conservation of the 1785–1786 plaster model commissioned by Jefferson. Displayed for many years in the rotunda of the State Capitol, the model was sent to the Colonial Williamsburg Foundation's conservation studios in 1994 for an assessment of its condition. The resulting research and conservation convinced the Library staff that the model deserved an exhibition that would explain its conception and conservation.

Co-curators F. Carey Howlett and Charles Brownell developed the exhibition to trace Jefferson's thinking about the role of a capitol building within the context of international interest in ancient temple structures. The exhibition afforded the curators the opportunity to incorporate new scholarship on Jefferson as an architect and his relationship with architectural draftsman Charles-Louis Clérisseau and *modeleur* Jean-Pierre Fouquet. The Library recognized that a revised and enlarged edition of Kimball's work needed to be published to include the findings of the conservators of the Fouquet model and to update the story of the Capitol as it stands today.

This new volume reprints not only the 1989 edition but also adds two essays that contribute to our appreciation of Fiske Kimball and our understanding of the Fouquet model. Charles Brownell's introduction discusses the strength of Kimball's scholarship on Jefferson and what new information or interpretations scholars have presented since Kimball. F. Carey Howlett's chapter presents an overview of the research and conservation of the Fouquet model from 1994 to 2001, drawn from Howlett's more-extensive article published in the winter 2002 issue of *Virginia Cavalcade*. The Colonial Williamsburg conservators, under Howlett's direction, made remarkable and unexpected discoveries during the conservation that raised as many questions as they answered, and the Library of Virginia is pleased to present those discoveries in this edition.

In its broadest scope, the Capitol Model Project included several components—research and conservation of the Fouquet model, creation of a new model to show how the Fouquet model arrived from Paris, the exhibition "Jefferson and the Capitol of Virginia" at the Library of Virginia and Colonial Williamsburg, a symposium at Colonial Williamsburg, and this revised and enlarged edition of Fiske Kimball's groundbreaking scholarship on Jefferson as the architect. The Library of Virginia thanks the Center for Palladian Studies in America, W. Bruce Wingo, Norfolk Southern Foundation, and the Library of Virginia Foundation for supporting this new edition of Kimball's pioneering work.

Many people and companies provided expertise, skill, and knowledge to the various components of the project: Aracor; William L. Beiswanger, The Thomas Jefferson Foundation, Monticello; Bob Berry, NASA; Charles E. Brownell, Virginia Commonwealth University; Tom Camden and Edward D. C. Campbell Jr., Library of Virginia; Geneviève Cuisset; Renee Davray-Piekolek; Helen Dorey, Sir John Soane's Museum, London, England; Conley Edwards III, Library of Virginia; Olivia Eller; Amy Fernandez, Colonial Williamsburg Foundation; Dr. Bruno Frohlich; James Murray Howard, University of Virginia; F. Carey Howlett; The Honorable Bruce F. Jamerson, House of Delegates, Commonwealth of Virginia; Audrey Johnson and Tracy Kamerer, Library of Virginia; Gary Guerin Lavarack; Scott Nolley; Bruce Pregger; Selden Richardson, Library of Virginia; Roland DGA Corporation; The Honorable Susan Clarke Schaar, The Senate of Virginia, Commonwealth of Virginia; Stanley Strong, Virginia Commonwealth University; Christopher Swan, Colonial Williamsburg Foundation; Werner Szambien; 3D Systems; Marjorie Trusted; John Watson, Carolyn J. Weekley, and Mark R. Wenger, Colonial Williamsburg Foundation; and James E. Wootton, Capitol Square Preservation Council.

The Library thanks Charles E. Brownell for his new introduction to this volume; Monica Rumsey for her editing skills; F. Carey Howlett for his guidance of and research into the conservation of the Fouquet model and for his essay in this volume; James E. Wootton for updating the epilogue; and, from the Library of Virginia, Gregg D. Kimball, Stacy G. Moore, Emily J. Salmon, and Brent Tarter for their editorial work and their assistance with writing the captions, Jennifer Davis McDaid for help with the bibliography, W. Paige Buchbinder and Pierre Courtois for their photography, and Amy C. Winegardner for her design of this edition.

BARBARA C. BATSON
LIBRARY OF VIRGINIA

Introduction to the 2002 Edition

"How is a taste for a chaste & good style of building to be formed in our countrymen unless we seize all occasions which the erection of public buildings offers, of presenting to them models for their imitation?"

Thomas Jefferson to Edmund Randolph
20 September 1785[1]

"The Capitol in the city of Richmond . . . is on the model of the temples of Erectheus at Athens, and of Balbec, and of the Maison quarrée of Nismes, all of which are nearly of the same form & proportions and are considered as the most perfect examples of Cubic architecture, as the Pantheon of Rome is of the Spherical."

Thomas Jefferson, "An Account of the Capitol in Virginia"[2]

fig. 2 Fiske Kimball, ca. 1915

In 1915 Fiske Kimball (1888–1955), one of the great architectural historians of the twentieth century, published his doctoral dissertation in three parts in the *Journal of the American Institute of Architects*. Kimball's article, entitled "Thomas Jefferson and the First Monument of the Classical Revival in America," established that Jefferson was the principal designer of the Virginia State Capitol, and Kimball's article gave Jefferson to the world as a major architect by international standards. Kimball's study remained the essential coverage of its subject for some seventy-five years. In 1989 the Virginia State Library and Archives (as the Library of Virginia was then called) adapted Kimball's article into an excellently edited book equipped with various additions to bring the story up-to-date. That convenient version of his work has promoted a transformation of the study of the Capitol, during the course of which much of Kimball's thinking has disintegrated. What did Kimball say, and how has the story changed in little more than a decade since the 1989 edition? This essay summarizes the new research.[3]

The title of Kimball's study—"Thomas Jefferson and the First Monument of the Classical Revival in America"—comes close to spelling out Kimball's goal. It seemed clear to him that the Capitol, shaped like a grand Roman temple on the outside, was the first American embodiment of the classicism that swept the architecture of the Western world in the late eighteenth and early nineteenth centuries. Like the building itself, the roles of Jefferson and his collaborator Charles-Louis Clérisseau in the creation of the Capitol had awaited systematic study. Having undertaken this study, Kimball concluded that Jefferson was "the real designer of this building, and thus the pioneer of our classical revival." He closed by asserting that "not merely in America, but in the development of modern classic architecture as a whole, the Virginia Capitol is

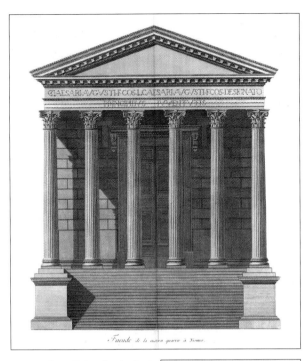

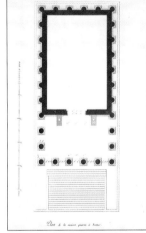

fig. 3 Maison Carrée, front elevation, from *Antiquités de la France*, by Charles-Louis Clérisseau, 1778, 2d edition, 1804. *fig. 4* Maison Carrée, plan, from *Antiquités de la France*.

a landmark of the first importance." (As an architect and critic, Kimball would develop the notion that Jefferson's Capitol had laid the basis for a distinctively American form of classicism appropriate for the twentieth century.)[4]

Kimball's study is a thing of beauty. It is the product of an intellect with remarkably advanced powers of analysis despite Kimball's youth (he published his article at the age of twenty-six), and one cannot read it without admiration. It is unfortunate that Kimball followed a principle that was very good to a conclusion that was very wrong. Great flaws in later publications on Jefferson's architecture have arisen from ignoring what the written documents say. In contrast, Kimball studied the written record faithfully, and he had no reason—or, rather, almost no reason—to reject Jefferson's own accounts of the creation of the Capitol design. Specifically, Kimball accepted Jefferson's statements that the design of the Capitol exterior originated in Jefferson's admiration for the temple called the Maison Carrée at Nîmes (dedicated ca. A.D. 4). At the same time, Kimball recognized that Jefferson's letters were, "to be sure, not wholly ingenuous, being colored by his desire to secure the adoption of the design."[5]

As faithfully as Kimball read what Jefferson wrote, he failed—even though he had been trained as an architect— to bring comparable penetration to another kind of document, the drawings for the Capitol that Jefferson made in Paris. Kimball arranged these drawings in what he saw as the convincing evolutionary sequence, beginning with the plans most like the Maison Carrée (fig. 4). Kimball did not recognize that these drawings, which he called the first project, showed more maturation than what he called the later plans (see fig. 28). More than a generation later, in 1949, Kimball identified two newly discovered Jefferson plans (fig. 29) as a pre-Parisian proposal for the Capitol. (We can call this proposal "Design 1.") Kimball dated the newfound project to 1780, to the preparations for removing the capital from Williamsburg to Richmond. He saw no reason to modify the evolutionary pattern that he had devised years earlier for Jefferson's Paris drawings.[6]

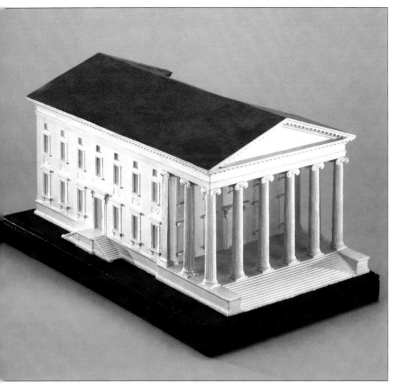
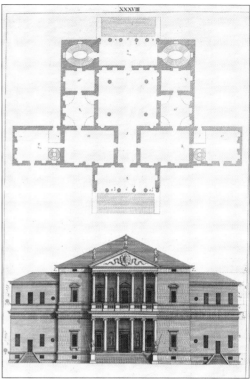

fig. 5 Model of the Virginia State Capitol by Jean-Pierre Fouquet, 1785–1786. *fig. 6* Front elevation and plan of the Villa Cornaro, from Book 2 of *The Architecture of A. Palladio*, edited by Giacomo Leoni, 2d edition, 1721.

In one respect, Kimball had followed poor procedure in 1915: he cited important evidence but ignored part of it. Kimball quoted the passage from Jefferson's "Account of the Capitol" that appears at the head of the present introduction, but wrote not a word to explain why Jefferson had said that the Richmond Capitol was on the model of an Athenian temple, the Erechtheum (fig. 13) at Athens (421–405 B.C.), and another temple at Balbec (or Baalbek) in Asia Minor (in what is now northeastern Lebanon) (fig. 14). Moreover, Kimball did not analyze Jefferson's goal of providing a model of "cubic architecture," to say nothing of "spherical architecture." This kind of omission should always raise suspicions that a story is very incomplete.[7]

In the 1989 State Library edition of Kimball's article, his work was reincarnated as a distinctly different publication. Kimball's new editors converted his study into an admirably careful, handy general architectural history of the Capitol. This publication, in book format, aligned Kimball's text with the scholarship since 1915, supplied fresh research, replaced his quotations with authoritative modern texts, abounded in added illustrations, and offered an irresistible alternative to the use of unlovely photocopies from an ancient journal. At the same time, Kimball's once-novel argument about the place of the design in history became almost undetectable.[8]

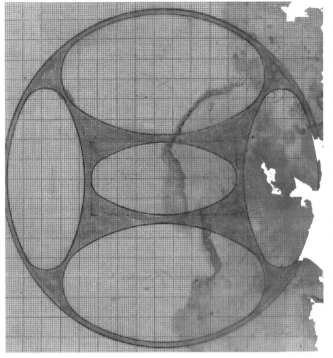

fig. 7 Thomas Jefferson's proposed plan for the United States Capitol, ca. 1791

The preparation of the 1989 edition brought with it the first suspicion that Kimball had erred by following Jefferson's writings at the expense of closely analyzing Jefferson's drawings. The challenge then arose that Kimball had put Jefferson's drawings into the wrong evolutionary sequence. This suspicion did not make its way into the book but would receive solid confirmation within two years.[9]

The years since 1989 have seen a stream of major disclosures germane to the Capitol, largely—although not quite entirely—by investigators who took advantage of the new version of Kimball. This outpouring began in 1990, with the work of three scholars, among whom pride of place belongs to a master who had by then studied Jefferson's architecture for more than a generation. At the Third Annual Symposium of the Department of Architectural History at the University of Virginia, Frank H. Sommer III offered a rich discussion of Jefferson's intellectual life as an architect. Sommer's arguments contrasted vividly with those of certain nonscholarly later-twentieth-century writers who, distorting Kimball's insights regarding Jefferson's French tastes, repeatedly attempted to align Jefferson with Parisian avant-garde architects in whom Jefferson in fact had no interest. Sommer instead identified Jefferson as a product of older classical movements, above all the British Palladianism of the early eighteenth century. Apropos of the Capitol, Sommer made a major contribution when he raised the question of why Jefferson had given a statehouse the form of a temple, a question that had been peculiarly neglected in print. Sommer demonstrated that Jefferson's books must have made him as aware as any modern classicist that the Romans often used temples as senate houses.[10]

The second contribution of 1990 addressed a question of attribution. To guide the builders of the Virginia Capitol, Jefferson sent a plaster model of his design from Paris (fig. 5). The Jefferson documents connect this model with men named Fouquet and Bloquet, and Kimball ascribed the making of the model to the latter. Geneviève Cuisset's 1990 study of Jean-Pierre Fouquet (1752–1829) and his son established the Fouquets as major makers of architectural models. Cuisset reassigned the Capitol model to the senior Fouquet, leaving one to suppose that Bloquet was a mere assistant.[11]

The third contribution of 1990 was Thomas J. McCormick's biography of Charles-Louis Clérisseau (1721–1820), which established Clérisseau as one of the great masters of architectural graphics. An internationally celebrated draftsman and an important teacher of architectural drawing, albeit only marginally an architect, Clérisseau was also a decorator and an authority on ornament. A further specialty of his was preparing corrected measured drawings of the Roman buildings published by the great North Italian architect Andrea Palladio (1508–1580) and the eminent French antiquary Antoine Desgodetz (1653–1728). A fraction of these drawings reached publication in Clérisseau's only book, *Antiquités de la France* (1778; see figs. 3–4), which played into the design of the Virginia Capitol.[12]

In mid-1991, the present author made the last changes to a summary of Jefferson scholarship for *The Making of Virginia Architecture*, a book published in 1992 by the Virginia Museum of Fine Arts in conjunction with its exhibition of the same name and year. The goal of those comments on Jefferson was to

  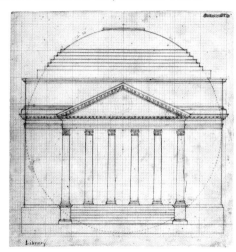

Left to right: *fig. 8* Front elevation of the Pantheon, in *Les Edifices Antiques de Rome* by Antoine Desgodetz, 1682; *fig. 9* Vitruvian Figures, from *Les Dix Livres d'Architecture de Vitruve*, edited by Claude Perrault, 2d edition, 1684; *fig. 10* Jefferson's front elevation of the Rotunda, University of Virginia, drawing begun in 1818.

summarize the best possible understanding of his architecture as of midsummer 1991, the last date for revising the manuscript. The Jefferson sections of the book developed Sommer's line of thought: Jefferson was a bookish devotee of Greco-Roman architecture as interpreted by certain "Moderns." These Moderns were above all Palladio (fig. 6) and certain of Palladio's seventeenth- and early-eighteenth-century disciples. Palladio's followers had made major changes to Palladio's legacy and, at the most recent, belonged to the defunct British Palladian movement of the earlier eighteenth century, not to any of the avant-garde of Jefferson's lifetime. It was a falsified British Palladian version of Palladio's treatise that Jefferson called the architectural "Bible." Jefferson depended on the three English editions published by Giacomo Leoni (ca. 1686–1746), a minor architect who drastically altered many of Palladio's illustrations to advertise his own services (see fig. 6).[13]

Apropos of the Virginia State Capitol, *The Making of Virginia Architecture* stressed Jefferson's own statements that he meant the building to serve as a model of cubic architecture. The book disclosed two designs for the national Capitol that had escaped previous researchers, one of them certainly by Jefferson (fig. 7) and one possibly attributable to him. The text argued that, after designing the Richmond statehouse as his model of cubic architecture, Jefferson strove to create a model of spherical architecture in Washington, on the example of the Pantheon in Rome (ca. A.D. 117–126/128; fig. 8). Jefferson's interest in proportions deriving from the square and the circle had a clear pedigree (fig. 9), back through the Palladians and Palladio to the first-century-B.C. Roman theorist Vitruvius, whom Jefferson had studied early in his architectural self-education. Jefferson finally succeeded in creating an example of spherical architecture with the University of Virginia Rotunda (construction was begun in 1823; fig. 10) where

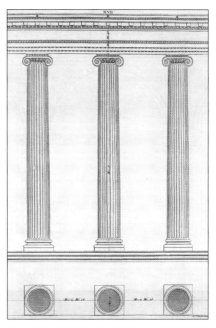

fig. 11 Ionic Order, from *The Architecture of A. Palladio,* edited by Giacomo Leoni, 2d edition, 1721

a stimulus from his friend B. Henry Latrobe (1764–1820) prompted him to rethink the Pantheon-style U.S. Capitol design.[14]

The Making of Virginia Architecture discussed another class of Jefferson's models. It proposed for the first time that Jefferson treated his buildings as "museums" of the Classical Orders—columns, their beams or entablatures, and related elements (fig. 11)—in the interest of setting models of those Orders for the reform of American architecture. To an extreme degree Jefferson subscribed to the traditional notion that the Orders were the principal ornament in architecture. In 1991, however, it was premature to apply this insight to the Virginia State Capitol.[15]

Indeed, my discussion of Jefferson ruefully acknowledged that Jefferson the architect remained an elusive topic. *The Making of Virginia Architecture* had to leave many major questions hanging. What exactly did Jefferson mean by "cubic" architecture? Why did Clérisseau write of his Capitol drawings that all of them "had to be done twice before they were drawn properly"? And why did Jefferson associate the Capitol design with the Erechtheum in Athens and a temple at Baalbek in Asia Minor?[16]

Events in the autumn of 1991 answered two of the dangling questions with the completion of "Jefferson's Design of the Capitol of Virginia," Brien J. Poffenberger's master's thesis at the University of Virginia. Poffenberger rediscovered two drafts and one set of notes for instructions that Jefferson wrote for Clérisseau. Kimball's wife, Marie Goebel Kimball, had published the first reference to these papers in 1950 without realizing their significance, and later writers had failed to pursue this important documentation.[17]

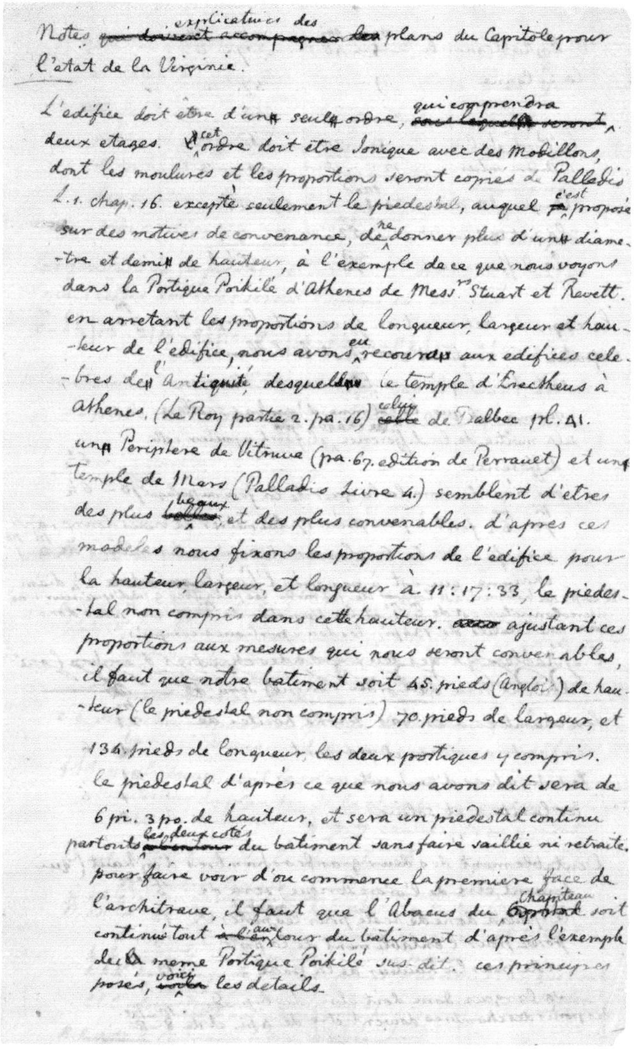
Notes explicatives des plans du Capitole pour l'etat de la Virginie.

L'edifice doit etre d'un seul ordre, qui comprendra deux etages. cet ordre doit etre Ionique avec des Mobillons, dont les moulures et les proportions seront copies de Palladio L. 1. chap. 16. excepté seulement le piedestal, auquel c'est proposé sur des motives de convenance, de ne donner plus d'un diametre et demi de hauteur, à l'exemple de ce que nous voyons dans la Portique Poikile d'Athenes de Messrs. Stuart et Revett. en arretant les proportions de longueur, largeur et hauteur de l'edifice, nous avons eu recours aux edifices celebres de l'antiquité desquels le temple d'Erectheus à athenes. (Le Roy partie 2. pa. 16) celui de Balbec pl. 41. un Periptere de Vitruve (pa. 67. edition de Perrault) et un temple de Mars (Palladio Livre 4.) semblent d'etres des plus beaux et des plus convenables. d'apres ces modeles nous fixons les proportions de l'edifice pour la hauteur, largeur, et longueur à 11 : 17 : 33, le piedestal non compris dans cette hauteur. ajustant ces proportions aux mesures qui nous seront convenables, il faut que notre batiment soit 45. pieds (Anglois) de hauteur (le piedestal non compris) 70. pieds de largeur, et 134. pieds de longueur, les deux portiques y compris. le piedestal d'après ce que nous avons dit sera de 6 pi. 3 po. de hauteur, et sera un piedestal continu partout les deux cotés du batiment sans faire saillie ni retraite. pour faire voir d'ou commence la premiere face de l'architrave, il faut que l'Abacus du Chapiteau soit continué tout autour du batiment d'après l'exemple de la meme Portique Poikile sus-dit. ces principes posés, voici les details.

fig. 12 Jefferson's "Notes explicatives des plans du Capitole pour l'état de la Virginie," 1785

The instructions to Clérisseau correspond with three sheets of Jefferson drawings and flesh them out (fig. 12). Providing clues to Jefferson's "cubic" system, the instructions tell us that Jefferson had turned to four temples in "fixing the proportions of length, breadth and height." Jefferson not only named the temples but also cited the books on which the design was to depend: "the temple of Erectheus [*sic*] in Athens (Le Roy, part 2, p. 16), that of Balbec pl. 41, a Peripter of Vitruvius (Perrault edition, p. 67,) and a temple of Mars (Palladio, Book 4)" (figs. 13–16). The specifications carefully enumerate the Orders that Jefferson wanted to display in this museum of the Orders. These documents nowhere mention the Maison Carrée, and the design called for in these specifications has nothing to do with that temple. The unearthing of this documentation made it clear that Kimball's sequence of designs was simply wrong.[18]

Focusing on the conceptions for the exterior, Poffenberger began the correct reconstruction of the evolution of the projects. We can clarify Poffenberger's argument by renaming Jefferson's schemes for the building as follows: Design 1 (fig. 29), as already noted, is the early proposal made in Virginia. Design 2 (figs. 31–33) is the first Paris proposal, externally echoing Design 1. Design 3 (figs. 34–37) is the second Paris proposal, externally reflecting the Maison Carrée.[19]

In other words, in Paris, when Jefferson responded to the Directors of the Public Buildings, he turned to Design 1, a temple with two porticoes, and modified it into Design 2. On the exterior, the change embodied the impact of newer archaeological literature. Clérisseau made a set of drawings of Design 2, but having just treated the Maison Carrée as a standard for ancient architecture in his own book, he talked Jefferson into revising the conception into Design 3. In this new version, the exterior became a temple with a deep portico at only one end, like the temple at Nîmes.

Clockwise from left: *fig. 13* Erechtheum, east elevation, from *Les Ruines des Plus Beaux Monuments de la Grèce,* by Julien-David Le Roy, 1758; *fig. 14* So-called Temple of Bacchus, perspective, from *The Ruins of Balbec,* by Robert Wood, 1757; *fig. 15* Peripteral temple, front elevation, from *Les Dix Livres d'Architecture de Vitruve,* edited by Claude Perrault, 1684; *fig. 16* "Temple of Mars" (Temple of Deified Hadrian), front elevation, from *The Architecture of A. Palladio,* edited by Giacomo Leoni, 2d edition, 1721.

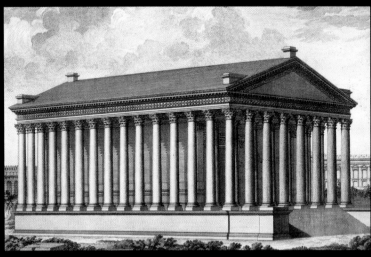

In 1993 two further contributions appeared. In honor of the 250th anniversary of Jefferson's birth, the editors of the *Virginia Magazine of History and Biography* devoted the January number of their journal to him, and they published a pair of articles by pathfinding scholars who reinforced each other's ideas. Douglas L. Wilson and Mark R. Wenger both concluded that Jefferson drew Design 1, not in 1780, at the time of the removal of the capital to Richmond, but in the early or mid-1770s. That is, as of the outset of the Revolution or even before, Jefferson had reached the idea of putting the rooms for the legislature inside a structure shaped like a temple. (Although neither author mentioned it, the planning of the interior of Design 1 was a glorified version of a house with a central passage.)[20]

Wenger further addressed a subject that previous writers had oddly ignored, Jefferson's planning of the rooms at the Capitol. Wenger's study is part of a larger scholarly development, the recent discovery that as an architect Jefferson drew profoundly on elements that he knew from Virginia custom, not just from European sources. Wenger brilliantly demonstrated that Jefferson's definitive room layout—seen in Design 2, Design 3, and the building as executed—adheres to the layout that Jefferson knew at the second Williamsburg Capitol (1751–1753), a layout largely established by the first Williamsburg Capitol (1701–1705).[21]

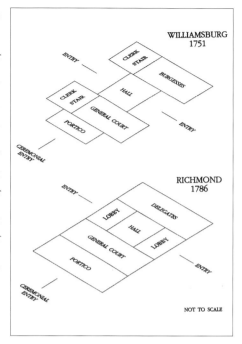

fig. 17 Comparative plans of the second Williamsburg Capitol and Jefferson's Design 3 for the Richmond Capitol, drawn by Mark R. Wenger, 1993

but into the side of the courtroom. Beyond the court lay a space for informal meetings. In the second Williamsburg Capitol as in Jefferson's later planning, this central space held a white marble statue of a memorable leader—Richard Hayward's figure of Lord Botetourt in Williamsburg (fig. 18), and, of course, Jean-Antoine Houdon's likeness of George Washington in the Richmond schemes (fig. 22). Past the central space came the chamber for the lower house of the legislature. The upper house was at the opposite end of the building, over the courtroom. This disposition contrasts vividly with another American arrangement that has become more familiar, the plan in which the upper and lower houses have balancing positions on the same floor.

In 1994, the year after the Wenger and Wilson articles, the present author made two contributions. My portions of the coauthored *Architectural Drawings of Benjamin Henry Latrobe* included a new analysis of the evolution of the "Temple Revival" that the Virginia Capitol inaugurated in American architecture. More central to the revision of Kimball's studies, work by my students was far enough along for me to sketch out fresh lines of study in the *Richmond Journal of History and Architecture*. The students in question

fig. 18 "View of Lord Botetourt's mutilated Statue Wmsburg," by B. Henry Latrobe, 1796, in the second Williamsburg Capitol

were Brian P. McRoberts, Ramin Saadat, and Joseph Senter White III, who presented their final results in the next few years.[22]

Brian McRoberts confronted an issue on which observers have not liked to dwell, the fact that the Capitol rotunda bears almost no resemblance to the central hall that evolved in Jefferson's floor plans and his remarks. During 1994–1995, in the absence of any Jefferson sectional drawing, McRoberts worked intensively from the evidence to reconstruct the hall of forty Palladian columns—twenty Ionic downstairs, twenty Corinthian upstairs—that Jefferson meant to surround the Houdon Washington as of Design 3. McRoberts got as far as a revised but still-preliminary reconstruction of this design for the rotunda, with two alternative treatments of the second-story guardrail (fig. 19). Sadly, McRoberts did not live to see the publication of his remarkably promising work.[23]

The second of the three students, Ramin Saadat, made a different, threefold contribution with his M.A. thesis on the Capitol (1994). Saadat showed, first, that Jefferson had applied Palladio's celebrated principles for the ideal temple to the Capitol, down to setting the building on top of a steep hill in a day when this siting did not spring from practicality. Secondly, Saadat isolated the source for the Design 3 rotunda in the ancient hypaethral temple, a temple open to the sky at the center. Jefferson knew this kind of temple from both Palladio (such as fig. 20) and Vitruvius.[24]

Thirdly, Saadat asked why Jefferson had devised a templelike exterior and a templelike core surrounding a white marble statue in a fashion suggesting divine honors. Saadat's answer, the theory of Euhemerism, holds great potential for future studies. Euhemerist theory argued that the ancient gods had in reality been mortal leaders or benefactors of the human race, and that, after their death, veneration of these men and women had naively evolved into worship. Euhemerism, named for the fourth-century Greek writer Euhemerus, flourished in the eighteenth century and probably holds a major key for interpreting the cult of George Washington in general. The theory can be traced to Jefferson's library with *The Chronology of Ancient Kingdoms Amended* (1728) by Isaac Newton, one of Jefferson's supreme heroes. By a Euhemerist reading, Washington, who gave his people liberty, would have deserved honors at least as great as those bestowed on any of the deified ancients, including a monumental edifice and a marble statue to carry his memory to later generations. It may follow that Jefferson saw the Virginia State Capitol as a "temple dedicated to the sovereignty of the people," a phrase that he later used to characterize the United States Capitol. In any case, the Euhemerist interpretation of Virginia's statehouse counteracts an old tendency not to recognize intellectual content in Jefferson's architecture.[25]

The last of the three students, Joseph Senter White III, brought his work on the Capitol to completion as a master's thesis in 1997. White made three durable contributions to the study of the Richmond statehouse. The first concerns the design that Jefferson's conception replaced (fig. 30). White argued persuasively that this project was meant to imitate the two-tiered Palladian portico of the second Williamsburg Capitol (fig. 21;

Left to right: *fig. 19* Tentative reconstruction of Jefferson's final conception for the rotunda of the Virginia State Capitol, drawn by Brian McRoberts in 1995; *fig. 20* "Temple of Jupiter" (Temple of Serapis), front elevation and section, from *The Architecture of A. Palladio*, edited by Giacomo Leoni, 2d edition, 1721.

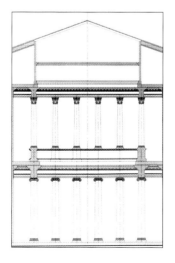

fig. 21 A nineteenth-century painting of the second Williamsburg Capitol, initialed "E.R.D."

compare fig. 6) but was to have four such porches. (White related this Capitol design to a line of Virginia build-ings with Palladian two-tiered porches that descended from the portico of the second Williamsburg Capitol.)[26]

In a second contribution, White argued convincingly that the executed rotunda, as one of the great American monumental interiors (fig. 22), derives from Cube Rooms, which Inigo Jones (1573–1652) had inaugurated as a British Palladian specialty (fig. 23). Although not a true cube, the rotunda takes one of the basic forms of the British Cube Room, with a gallery cantilevered on scrolled brackets halfway up the wall. Someone—almost certainly the Richmond architect Samuel Dobie (d. 1801)—gave the Richmond space a dome that is not usually found on Cube Rooms in Britain.[27]

As a third contribution, White demonstrated a major, easily documented point that Kimball and his successors had overlooked. Jefferson impractically placed the Capitol offices on a lofty third floor, in the heat under the roof, up many stairs. In execution, someone, very likely Dobie, moved these offices to a more usable location down in the Capitol podium, which was raised higher to hold them and was stripped of Jefferson's front steps so that the offices could have windows (fig. 24).[28]

In 1999 the present author added to the interpretation of Virginia's Capitol with the publication of a 1993 conference paper, "Thomas Jefferson's Architectural Models and the United States Capitol." The essay argued first and foremost that, as much as any other individual, Jefferson was one of the architects of the United States Capitol, and, secondarily, that Jefferson shaped the building largely by promoting models for other architects to imitate. Addressing the most important of these models, the essay provided the first full-dress study of Jefferson's custom of treating buildings as museums of the Orders to promote the reform of American architecture. As is well known, Jefferson documented this intention in the case of his culminating work, the University of Virginia (construction begun in 1817; fig. 25). (For instance, in one famous passage, he wrote to Latrobe in 1817 that he meant the University pavilions to "serve as specimens of the orders for the architectural lectures.") "Jefferson's Models" tracked this didactic use of the Orders from the conception for the first Monticello (begun in 1769) through Virginia's statehouse and the second Monticello (begun in 1796) to the national Capitol (1793–1829). The essay explained that Jefferson meant to achieve his reforms by grafting his models onto the long-standing practice of basing new construction on extant buildings, often by means of a contract. On the subject of Richmond, the paper analyzed the Palladian set of Orders that Jefferson specified for Design 2 and probably still intended for Design 3. The essay used the tentative McRoberts reconstruction of the center hall to illustrate the internal climax of the suite of Orders (fig. 19).[29]

Top: *fig. 22* The rotunda of the Virginia State Capitol from the southwest; Bottom: *fig. 23* The Great Hall of the Queen's House from the southeast, Greenwich, England, Inigo Jones, begun in 1616.

The essay made two further contributions to the study of the Virginia State Capitol. First, it marshaled conclusive evidence against the unfounded misconception that Jefferson sought to revive Roman Republican models as the basis for the architecture of the young American Republic. Generally, as the essay put it, "the 'republican' interpretation of Jefferson's architecture does not have a leg to stand on." Specifically, Jefferson again and again acknowledged that the Maison Carrée dated to the Roman Imperial period—"the time of the Caesars"—and, indeed, he admiringly used Roman Imperial models until the very end of his career.[30]

The "Jefferson's Models" conference paper made a second contribution by showing how Jefferson made the United States Capitol a sequel to his Virginia Capitol. With two of the Washington chambers this is clear. In 1808–1810 when Latrobe rebuilt the interior of the east side of the national Capitol's North Wing, he executed Jefferson's idea of putting a courtroom beneath the Senate chamber (fig. 26). He reconstituted this plan after the burning of the Capitol in 1814. This arrangement of two of the three great chambers in the national statehouse is an obvious outgrowth of Jefferson's interest in the second Williamsburg Capitol plan and of his reinterpretation of this plan for the Richmond Capitol.

With another of the Washington interiors, the rotunda, the relation to Richmond is less certain. A decisive conception that appeared in the planning of the national Capitol as early as 1793 was the idea of a white marble statue of George Washington in a templelike space at the center of the building. The notion—realized briefly in the years 1841–1843 when a monumental figure of Washington by Horatio Greenough sat in the rotunda—has a pregnant similarity to Designs 2 and 3, as well as a likeness to the plan of the second Williamsburg Capitol. "Jefferson's Models" raised the question of whether this idea of a rotunda with a Washington monument stemmed from Jefferson, then serving as the United States secretary of state, who concerned himself deeply with the design of the federal Capitol from the outset, sometimes working very effectively behind the scenes.

fig. 24 The Virginia State Capitol from the west, 1801, from a drawing by Lawrence Sully, engraved by Alexander Lawson

The year 2001 closed with the finish of one of the most important of all investigations into the design of the Capitol, the conservation of the Fouquet model (fig. 5) by F. Carey Howlett at the Colonial Williamsburg

fig. 25 The University of Virginia from the south, drawn by Ennion Williams and engraved by Benjamin Tanner in 1826.

Foundation. For the conservator's own account of this effort, see "Revealing Jefferson's Model for the Capitol of Virginia" following Kimball's 1915 essay in this book. This undertaking and the attendant attempt to create a duplicate of the model as it looked in perhaps the second stage of its existence have produced a series of revelations. The discoveries in turn entail questions that will occupy researchers for years to come. The new findings create yet more distance between Fiske Kimball and us; indeed, it might well be that a full study of the model would now run to the same length as Kimball's original article on the Capitol. Amid all the information now available, two points stand out. First, because we now know the almost inconceivable perfection of detail that lies buried under some fifteen coats of paint (fig. 27), we can for the first time understand why Jefferson went to the lengths of commissioning a plaster model. He meant that model to direct the builders in minute detail, a circumstance that one previously could not envision from the painted model's lumpish surfaces. The second great result of Howlett's work is to reveal the model to us as an elegant and captivating work of art in its own right.

So it is that, with the 1989 reprint of Kimball's text to facilitate research, in about a decade we have traveled a long way from Fiske Kimball, who after all embarked on his Jeffersonian researches the better part of

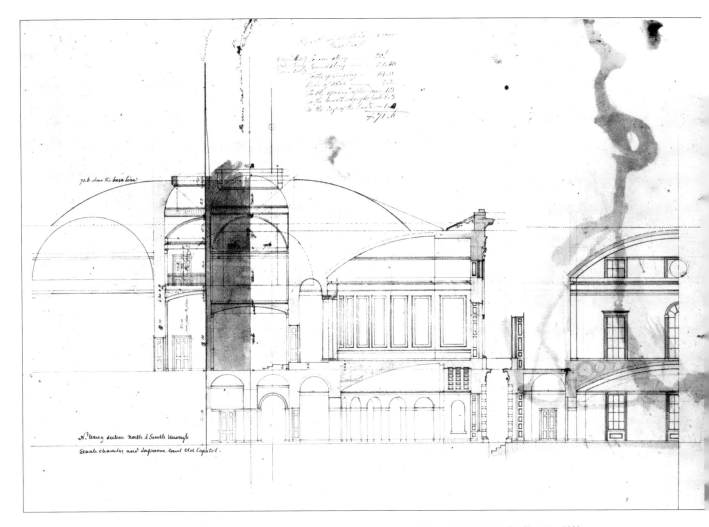

fig. 26 Studies for the courtroom and Senate chamber in the United States Capitol, by B. Henry Latrobe, probably begun before November 1806

a hundred years ago. Still, our own journey has far to go. In 2002–2003, the exhibition "Jefferson and the Capitol of Virginia"—at the Library of Virginia in Richmond and at the DeWitt Wallace Decorative Arts Museum in Colonial Williamsburg—allows us to evaluate our progress. We have a much better understanding of the evolution of the Jeffersonian and non-Jeffersonian conceptions for the big building on Shockoe Hill, and we have a much better understanding of the sequels in American architecture. And yet we do not have anything like an adequate history of the construction of the Virginia State Capitol. We know a great deal about the lessons that Jefferson adopted from European culture, particularly about his reliance on older rather than avant-garde architectural thought, and we know something about the American customs that he embraced, such as the deliberate habit of basing new buildings on standing ones. Even so, Jefferson's major models can be puzzling: What did he mean by calling the Virginia State Capitol an exemplar of cubic architecture? How did he arrive at the principal exhibit in his intended museum of the Orders, the unusual Ionic Order on the Fouquet model? We have begun to understand Jefferson's interest in the lore of the temple and apotheosis, but only just begun. If at last we know why Clérisseau made two sets of renderings for the Richmond temple, and if we have learned much about Fouquet's model and Jefferson's drawings, the fact remains that we have only the most summary ideas about the evolution of those drawings, and, hence, about the workings of Jefferson's mind as his design grew. We do have much to learn.[31]

fig. 27 A reverse X ray of the garland ornamentation on Fouquet's model of the Virginia State Capitol brings to light his exquisitely detailed artisanry.

Clearly, then, we cannot afford to view Kimball with complacent superiority. Standing behind us down the road, he remains an inspiring figure because of his sheer ability. Moreover, with all that has altered in the interpretation of Jefferson and his statehouse, Kimball's contribution has by no means evaporated. We still owe to Fiske Kimball the recognition that Jefferson was the principal designer of the Virginia State Capitol, the recognition that the Capitol is a major building by international standards, and the recognition that Thomas Jefferson, architect, rather than belonging to a narrower history, has a distinguished place in the annals of world architecture.

CHARLES BROWNELL
VIRGINIA COMMONWEALTH UNIVERSITY

KIMBALL SEQUENCE

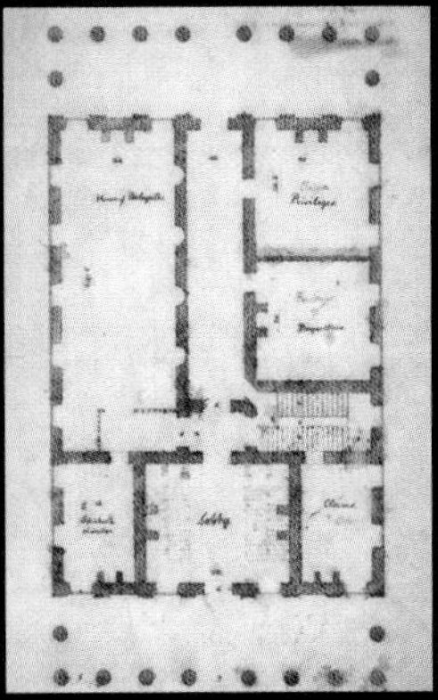

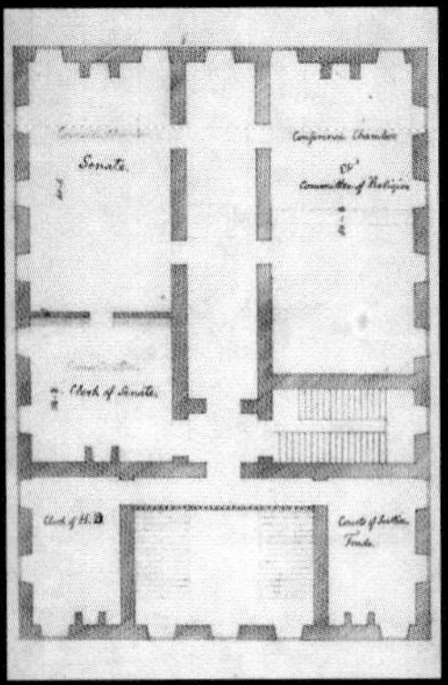

Directors' Plan

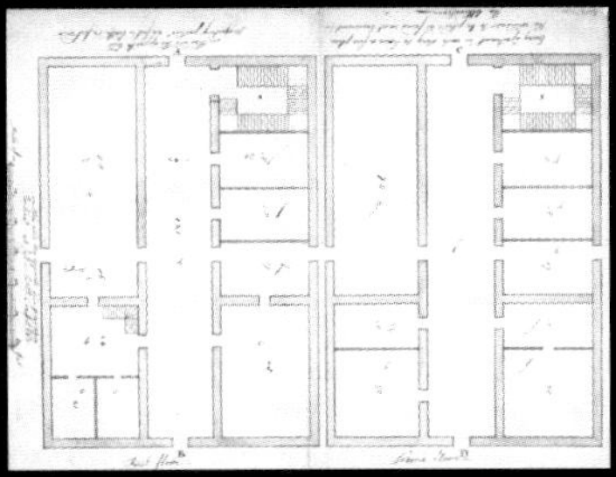

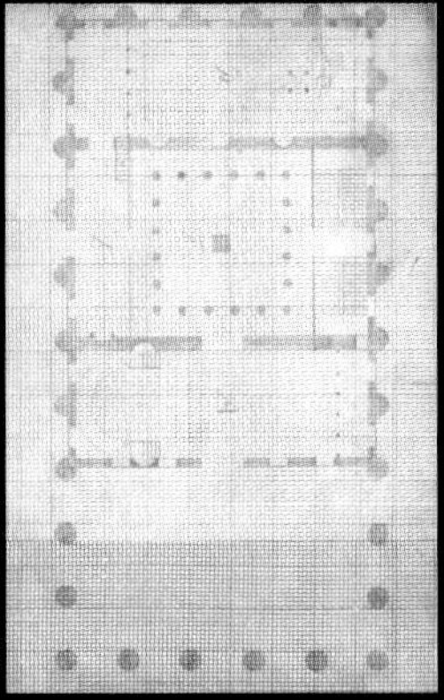

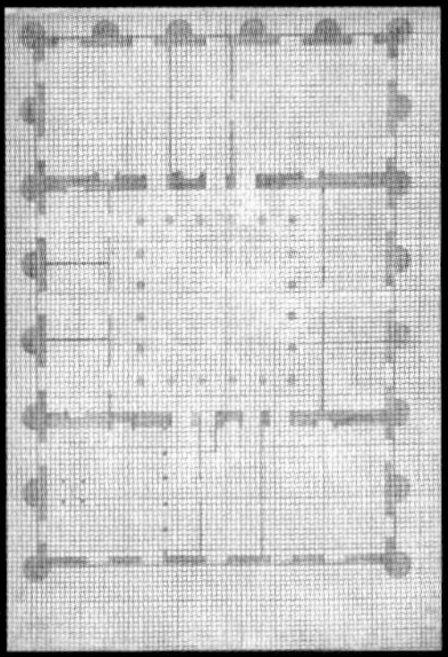

Plan 2

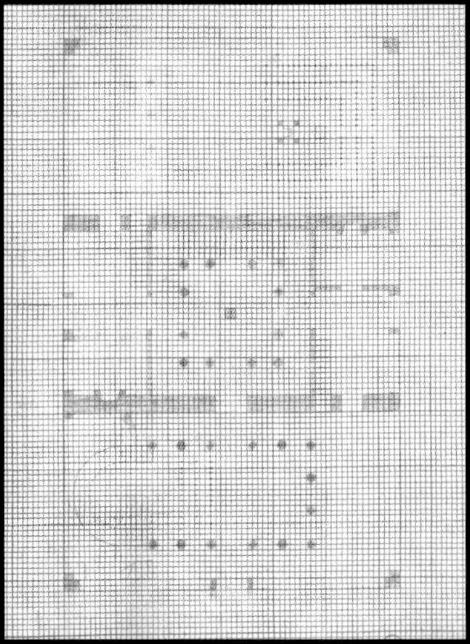

BROWNELL SEQUENCE

Design 1

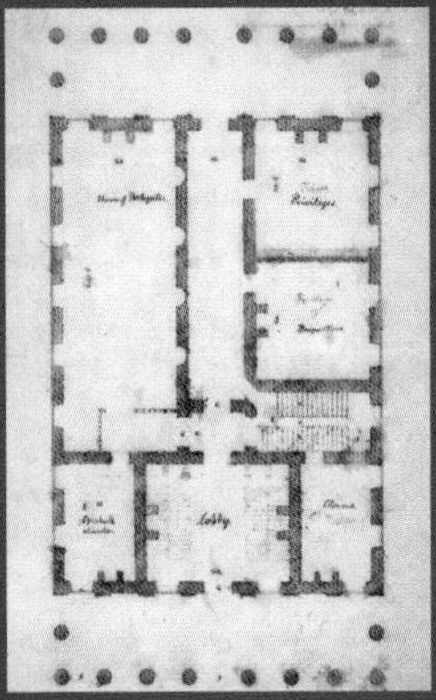

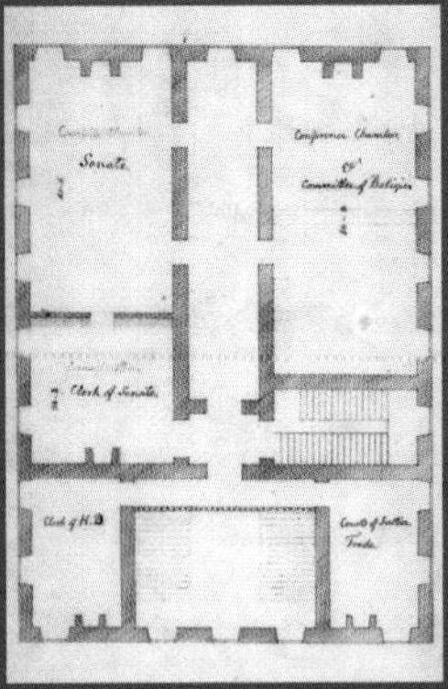

Directors' Plan

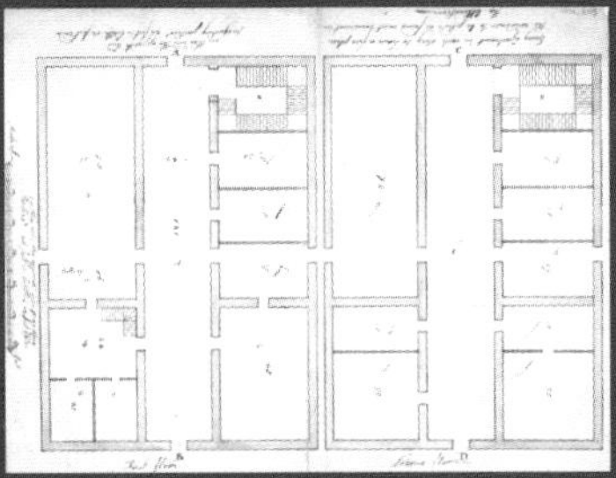

Design 2—Early Phase

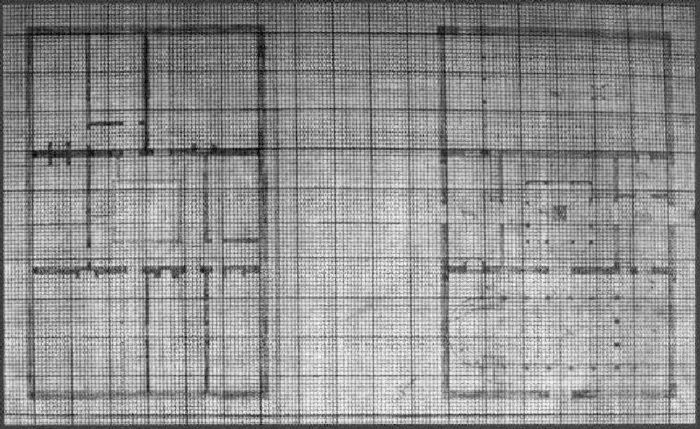

Design 2—
Later Phase

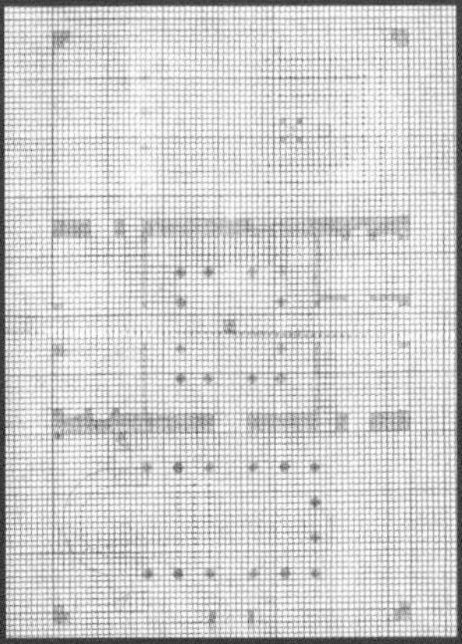

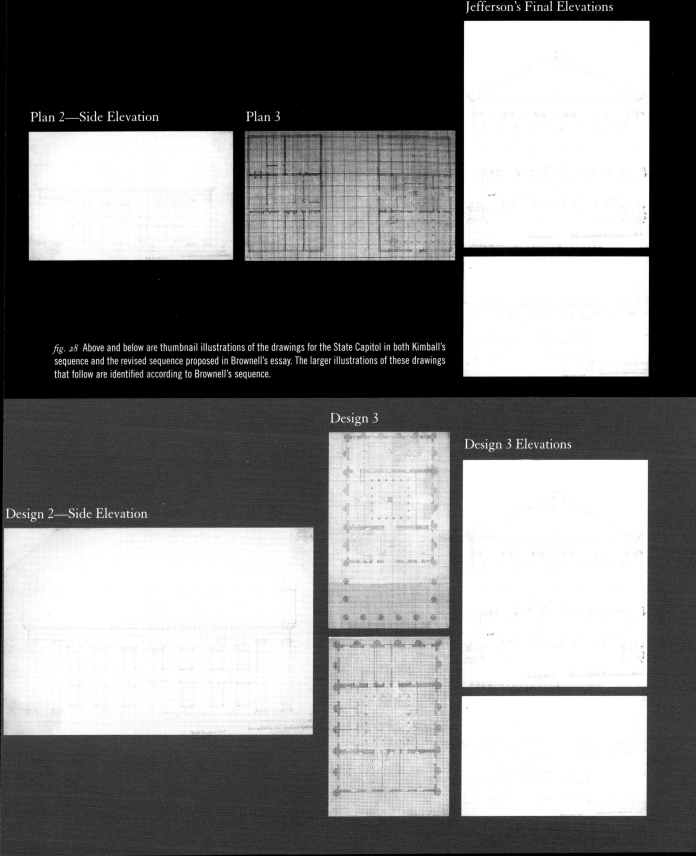

Jefferson's Final Elevations

Plan 2—Side Elevation

Plan 3

fig. 28 Above and below are thumbnail illustrations of the drawings for the State Capitol in both Kimball's sequence and the revised sequence proposed in Brownell's essay. The larger illustrations of these drawings that follow are identified according to Brownell's sequence.

Design 3

Design 3 Elevations

Design 2—Side Elevation

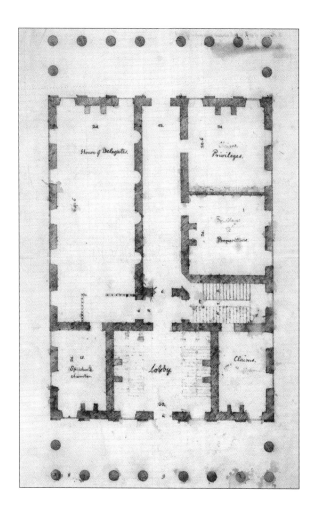
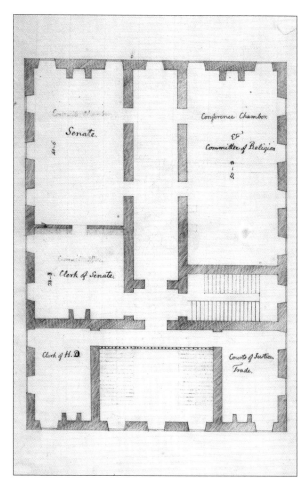

fig. 29 Jefferson's Design 1 for the State Capitol, plans of the first and second floors, drawn in the early or mid-1770s

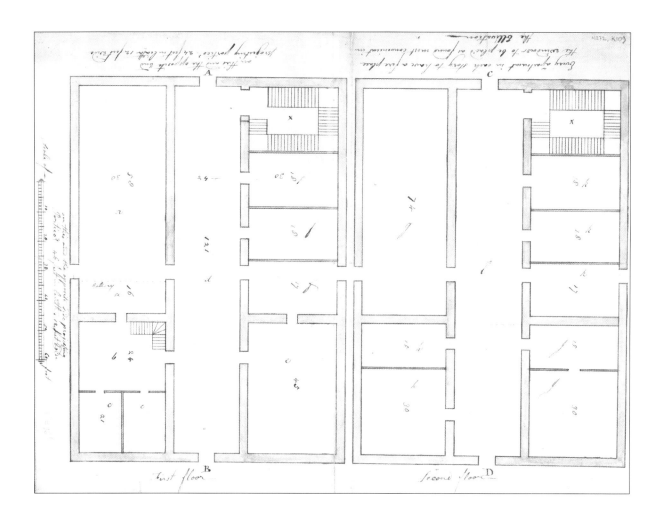

fig. 30 The Directors' design of the first and second floors for the State Capitol, possibly by Ryland Randolph, 1785

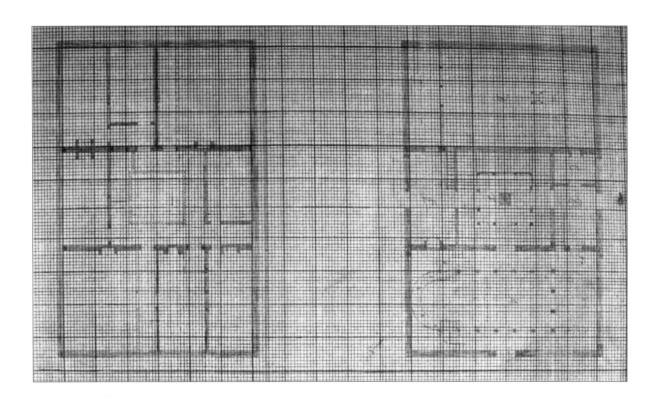

fig. 31 Jefferson's Design 2 for the State Capitol, early plans of the first and second floors, 1785

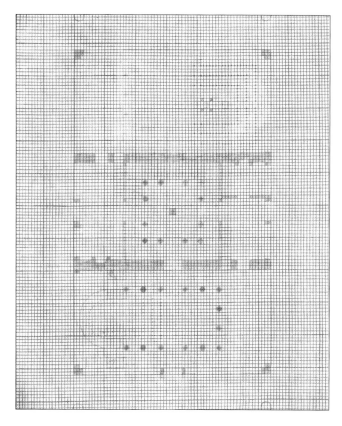

fig. 32 Jefferson's Design 2 for the State Capitol, later plan of the first floor, 1785. *fig. 33* Jefferson's Design 2 for the State Capitol, side elevation, 1785.

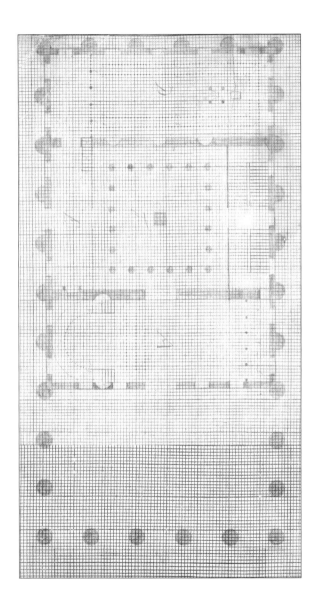
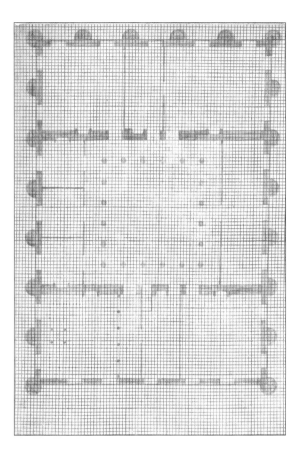

fig. 34 Jefferson's Design 3 for the State Capitol, plan of the first floor, 1785. *fig. 35* Design 3 for the State Capitol, plan of second floor, 1785.

fig. 36 Design 3 for the State Capitol, side elevation by Thomas Jefferson with details by Charles-Louis Clérisseau, 1785. *fig. 37* Design 3 for the State Capitol, front elevation by Thomas Jefferson with details by Charles-Louis Clérisseau, 1785.

Foreword to the 1989 Edition

The Capitol of Virginia has served the citizens of the commonwealth since Speaker Thomas Mathews called the House of Delegates to order in its new chamber on 27 October 1788. A preeminent landmark of the Old Dominion, the Capitol has witnessed many great events in the history of the commonwealth and the nation. The original building, designed by Thomas Jefferson and augmented in 1904–1906 with wings to the east and west, is home to the General Assembly of Virginia, the oldest continuous representative assembly in the New World.

Virginia's many contributions to America are proclaimed throughout the building. Since 1796 Houdon's magnificent statue of George Washington has stood in the rotunda, surrounded today by the busts of seven other Virginia-born presidents of the United States—Thomas Jefferson, James Madison, James Monroe, William Henry Harrison, John Tyler, Zachary Taylor, and Woodrow Wilson. Nearby is the Old Hall of the House of Delegates, meeting place of Virginia's Secession Convention and of the Confederate Congress, where a full-length statue of Robert E. Lee marks the spot on which he formally accepted command of the Army of Northern Virginia on 23 April 1861. In the halls and meeting rooms of the Capitol, portraits and memorials remind schoolchildren and veteran legislators alike of their heritage and responsibilities.

The General Assembly of Virginia has proudly celebrated the 200th anniversary of the Capitol of Virginia. In 1985 the General Assembly sponsored public festivities in Capitol Square marking the laying of the cornerstone for the new Capitol on 18 August 1785, and in 1988 several leaders of the House and Senate donned eighteenth-century garb to commemorate their predecessors' initial meetings in the new building with a ceremonial reenactment of the move from Shockoe Slip to Shockoe Hill. The journals of the General Assembly record that the House of Delegates (meeting for the last time in the old tobacco warehouse at the corner of Fourteenth and Cary Streets that served as Virginia's temporary statehouse) on Saturday, 25 October 1788, had resolved "that when this House adjourns this day, it will adjourn to the apartments prepared for the use of the General Assembly, in the new Capitol on Shockoe Hill." The House of Delegates gathered in the new Capitol for the first time on that Monday, the twenty-seventh, and on Wednesday, the twenty-ninth, the Senate first met in its new chamber.

The General Assembly's celebrations of the 200th of the Capitol have been directed by a joint subcommittee whose members were Hunter B. Andrews, Stuart B. Fallen, James T. Latimer, Bruce MacDougal, C. Hardaway Marks, Thomas W. Moss, Jr., William F. Parkerson, Jr., and A. L. Philpott. In connection with these festivities in 1985 and 1988, the General Assembly also sponsored this new edition of Fiske Kimball's classic study of the Capitol. We are grateful to the late Donald Haynes, State Librarian from 1972 to 1986, and his successor, Ella Gaines Yates, for their support and for the assistance of the library staff and especially of historian Jon Kukla.

Americans today are familiar with Jefferson's talents for architecture but prior to the publication in 1915 of Kimball's studies, Jefferson and his role in designing the Capitol after the Maison Carrée were not generally recognized. Kimball's original monograph, which has long been out of print, established these facts beyond any doubt. This new edition, illustrated with historic drawings and prints as well as color and black-and-white photographs, makes Kimball's pathbreaking scholarship accessible once again and is a fitting and lasting tribute to a great American landmark.

A. L. PHILPOTT, SPEAKER
VIRGINIA HOUSE OF DELEGATES

Editorial Note to the 1989 Edition

This edition of Fiske Kimball's *Capitol of Virginia: A Landmark of American Architecture* is based on the text he published as "Thomas Jefferson and the First Monument of the Classical Revival in America" in the *Journal of the American Institute of Architects* in 1915. The editors thoroughly reviewed that text and examined—in manuscript, microform, or print—both the sources Kimball had consulted and others that have become available since 1915. The editors traced Kimball's quotations to definitive modern editions or the original manuscripts, thereby confirming the precision of his research and adjusting his quoted texts to accepted practices of modern documentary editing—using Julian P. Boyd et al., eds., *The Papers of Thomas Jefferson*, 29 vols. to date (Princeton, 1950–), as the preferred source for Jefferson's correspondence and (with one exception) original manuscripts in the Archives Branch of the Virginia State Library and Archives for texts that Kimball quoted from William P. Palmer et al., eds., *Calendar of Virginia State Papers and Other Manuscripts Preserved in the Capitol at Richmond, 1652–1869*, 11 vols. (Richmond, 1875–1893).

During his productive career Kimball often wrote engagingly for wide audiences, but in many places the 1915 text for this book betrayed its academic lineage: the newly minted Ph.D. penned several arduous sentences and was sometimes overly cautious when stating conclusions that today are widely accepted as a result of his scholarship. Throughout this posthumous edition, where required for greater clarity or directness, the editors have amended or amplified Kimball's prose. His opening survey of nineteenth-century scholarship was omitted for the reasons suggested in the Introduction. This second edition provides a paragraph at page 4 about drawings in the Huntington Library that Kimball treated in a journal article in the 1940s, as well as a brief epilogue sketching the architectural history of the Capitol in the twentieth century. Linda J. Pike, of Cornell University, translated most of the French quotations that Kimball published. Inventory numbers (Kl09–Kl17) assigned by Kimball in *Thomas Jefferson, Architect: Original Designs in the Coolidge Collection of the Massachusetts Historical Society* (Boston, 1916; reprint, New York, 1968) and checklist numbers (N270–N280) assigned by Frederick Doveton Nichols in *Thomas Jefferson's Architectural Drawings, with Commentary and a Check List* (Boston, 1960; 2d ed., Charlottesville, 1961), 31–44, are printed in the credit lines accompanying Jefferson's drawings and Jean-Pierre Fouquet's model.

ACKNOWLEDGMENTS

The Honorable A. L. Philpott, Speaker of the House of Delegates, and the members of his joint subcommittee—Hunter B. Andrews, Stuart B. Fallen, James T. Latimer, Bruce MacDougal, C. Hardaway Marks, Thomas W. Moss, Jr., and William F. Parkerson, Jr.—supported and encouraged this edition from its inception, as did Carol S. Headley, administrative assistant to the Speaker. Editorial advice from Emily J. Salmon was invaluable. John S. Robertson, librarian of the Fiske Kimball Fine Arts Library at the University of

Virginia, Suzanne Hill Freeman, of the James Branch Cabell Library at Virginia Commonwealth University, and Joseph D. Lahendro, architect, of Richmond, graciously contributed information about Fiske Kimball. Kimberly Prothro, Jack Boucher, and Nancy Harrington generously shared material from the Historic American Buildings Survey.

Introduction to the 1989 Edition

Fiske Kimball was twenty-seven years old in the autumn of 1915 when installments of his study of the Capitol of Virginia graced three successive issues of the *Journal of the American Institute of Architects* under the title "Thomas Jefferson and the First Monument of the Classical Revival in America." Kimball's essay was a product of his doctoral research and, like many others written by young scholars, it began with his summary of the inadequate state of scholarship about the Capitol of Virginia. Of course, he readily admitted, there was no doubt that the Capitol had been designed "in conscious imitation of the Maison Carrée." Neither was there any dispute about its seniority as the first Classical Revival building in America; the Capitol stood essentially complete in 1789 when the nation's second Classical Revival edifice arose on Boston's Beacon Hill, the triumphal column monument designed by Charles Bulfinch. Neither of these facts was in doubt in 1915, but Kimball knew that "the building itself and the question of its authorship" had never received careful study. Although it was "well known that Thomas Jefferson and the French architect, Clérisseau, each had a share in its design, the exact nature and relative extent of their services" had never been defined. Kimball had set out to "establish, beyond much dispute, the real designer of this building, and thus the pioneer of our classical revival in architecture."[1] Today, the telling measure of Kimball's success is the fact that for seven decades architectural historians and the general public alike have accepted his persuasive explanations and relied on his exacting scholarship, as published in the original version of this book and, a year later, in his pioneering *Thomas Jefferson: Architect* (Boston, 1916). Today's commonplace truths—that Jefferson designed the Capitol of Virginia and that architecture was a notable manifestation of Jefferson's genius—are among the legacies of Fiske Kimball's contributions to American architectural history. This new edition of Kimball's work, sponsored by the General Assembly of Virginia in celebration of the 200th anniversary of the Capitol, is a fitting commemoration of the building and its foremost historian.

Born in Newton, Massachusetts, in 1888 and graduated summa cum laude from Harvard University in 1909, Sidney Fiske Kimball submitted his pathbreaking study of the Capitol of Virginia as his doctoral dissertation at the University of Michigan in 1915. He taught at the Universities of Illinois and Michigan from 1912 to 1918, and he chaired the new University of Virginia School of Architecture from 1918 to 1923, when he accepted appointment at New York University as chairman of the Department of Fine Arts and Morse Professor of the Literature of the Arts of Design. In 1925 Kimball began his thirty-year career as director of the Philadelphia Museum of Art, which he transformed from an "empty shell into one of the greatest museums of the world," before his resignation, in diminished health, in January 1955 and his death that August at the age of seventy-seven.[2]

Kimball and his wife, Marie Goebel Kimball, were avid students of Thomas Jefferson and the Old Dominion. His works established Jefferson's place in the history of American architecture,[3] and she published three volumes of a detailed biography of Jefferson,[4] but their contributions to the interpretation of Virginia history were not exclusively confined to books. As a practicing architect Kimball designed Shack Mountain in Charlottesville, Scottwood in Ann Arbor, and several building projects on the grounds of the University of Virginia. In the field of historic preservation, Kimball's advice shaped the initial restorations of Williamsburg, Stratford, Gunston Hall, and especially Monticello. "A perceptive critic and a leader in the study of eighteenth-century architecture," Fiske Kimball "combined a broad historical view with unusual daring and a sharp ability to discover the unknown"—qualities as evident in the genius of his career as in the enduring scholarship of his first monograph.[5]

JON KUKLA
VIRGINIA STATE LIBRARY AND ARCHIVES

THE *Capitol* of VIRGINIA

A LANDMARK OF AMERICAN ARCHITECTURE

A New Capitol

The story of the Virginia Capitol at Richmond starts with Thomas Jefferson's draft of the Bill for the Removal of the Seat of Government of Virginia, presented to the House of Delegates on 11 November 1776. This was the first proposal in any of the independent American states to make adequate provisions for the new form of government.[1] As revised and passed by the General Assembly in 1779, the act provided

> that six whole squares of ground surrounded each of them by four streets . . . shall be appropriated to the use and purpose of publick buildings: On one of the said squares shall be erected, one house for the use of the general assembly, to be called the capitol, which said capitol shall contain two apartments for the use of the senate and their clerk, two others for the use of the house of delegates and their clerk, and others for the purposes of conferences, committees and a lobby, of such forms and dimensions as shall be adopted to their respective purposes: On one other of the said squares shall be erected, another building to be called the halls of justice, . . . and on the same square last mentioned shall be built a publick jail: One other of the said squares shall be reserved for the purpose of building thereon hereafter, a house for the several executive boards and offices to be held in: Two others with the intervening street, shall be reserved for the use of the governour of this commonwealth for the time being, and the remaining square shall be appropriated to the use of the publick market. The said houses shall be built in a handsome manner with walls of brick or stone, and porticoes where the same may be convenient or ornamental, and with pillars and pavements of stone.[2]

For the selection of grounds, the choice of plans and building materials, five persons to be called the Directors of the Public Buildings were to be appointed by the assembly.

Although the bill failed of passage in 1776, a revised bill was introduced in 1779 and passed, making Richmond the capital after the last day of April 1780. The May 1780 act for locating the public buildings on Shockoe Hill, passed in the first session of the assembly held at Richmond, named nine Directors, beginning with his excellency Thomas Jefferson, then governor of the commonwealth.[3] The importance of Jefferson's proposals from the architectural standpoint lies in the provision for separate buildings for the legislative, judicial, and executive branches of the government, the executive building being for the several executive boards and offices, and distinct from the governor's residence. Such a strict division was hitherto unknown in America, and indeed in Europe. European governments generally were not organized in such a way as to permit this separation; they occupied for the most part remodeled palaces not specifically designed for their functions. The colonial capitols or statehouses had contained all three branches of their governments, and this arrangement was continued when the states become independent. In Virginia the colony's General Court, which had consisted of the governor and Council, held its sessions in the General Court's room on the first floor of the Capitol in Williamsburg. The old courthouse of 1770 at Williamsburg was used only by the town and the county, and the Governor's Palace, of course, did not correspond to the executive building that Jefferson proposed. Under the state government, although an independent judiciary was organized, its courts still convened in the Capitol while the government remained at Williamsburg. Jefferson's scheme, as enacted, would have produced not merely a monumental grouping new to America, but individual buildings of a novel character, anticipating in type the great independent parliament buildings and *palais de justice* of modern Europe.

The General Assembly elected Virginia's first five Directors of the Public Buildings on 24 June 1779: James Buchanan, Archibald Cary, Robert Goode, Robert Carter Nicholas, and Turner Southall. The legislature named four more Directors in May 1780—Richard Adams, Samuel DuVal, Thomas Jefferson, and Edmund Randolph—and four years later appointed Jacquelin Ambler and William Hay to vacancies created by the deaths of Nicholas and DuVal. The 1779 legislation did not specify the buildings' location within Richmond, and as late as December 1779 Senate Speaker Archibald Cary asked Jefferson, "Have they determined on which Hill to build"? Cary's question was answered by the 1780 statute, which placed the government buildings on Shockoe Hill. Jefferson's extant drawings from these years of deliberation include street maps for Richmond and Shockoe Hill and sketches for separate buildings for the branches of government: a hall of justice, a governor's residence, and a capitol. In the spring or summer of 1780, after relocating in Richmond and becoming a Director himself, Jefferson made large drawings for a temple-form building to accommodate the House of Delegates, Senate, clerks, and legislative committees. These two drawings, which are preserved at the Huntington Library, affirm that Jefferson had determined the fundamental scheme of the Capitol before he left America and long before he met Charles-Louis Clérisseau, who helped him in France.[4]

The plan for separate buildings, embodied in the legislation passed in 1780, was beyond the ideas and resources of the time. No sooner had Jefferson left the country as minister plenipotentiary to France than the law was modified. An act passed at the session of October 1784 provided that

> Whereas it hath been represented to the general assembly, by the directors of the public buildings, that apartments can be provided for the use of the legislative, executive, and judiciary, to greater advantage, and with less expense, by uniting them under one roof, than by erecting separate houses; . . . That it shall be in the discretion of the said directors to cause apartments to be provided for the uses aforesaid under one and the same roof; any law to the contrary notwithstanding.[5]

The proposal for independent buildings was thus stillborn, and the colonial precedent, still closely followed in America, was perpetuated.

The familiar account of Jefferson's later connection with the building of the Virginia Capitol is the one given in his memoir, set down in 1821:

> I was written to in 1785 (being then in Paris) by directors appointed to superintend the building of a Capitol in Richmond, to advise them as to a plan, and to add to it one of a Prison. Thinking it a favorable opportunity of introducing into the State an example of architecture, in the classic style of antiquity, and the Maison Quarrée of Nismes, an ancient Roman temple, being considered as the most perfect model existing of what may be called Cubic architecture, I applied to M. Clerissault, who had published drawings of the Antiquities of Nismes, to have me a model of the building made in stucco, only changing the order from Corinthian to Ionic, on account of the difficulty of the Corinthian capitals. I yielded, with reluctance, to the taste of Clerissault, in his preference of the modern capital of Scamozzi to the more noble capital of antiquity. This was executed by the artist whom Choiseul Gouffier had carried with him to Constantinople, and employed, while Ambassador there, in making those beautiful models of the remains of Grecian architecture which are to be seen at Paris. To adapt the exterior to our use, I drew a plan for the interior, with the apartments necessary for legislative, executive, and judiciary purposes; and accommodated in their size and distribution to the form and dimensions of the building. These were forwarded to the Directors, in 1786, and were carried into execution, with some variations, not for the better, the most important of which, however, admit of future correction.[6]

Among the letters Jefferson wrote, urging delay until the plans should arrive from abroad, are several passages that might have been expected to give a hint about his own part in their preparation. They have the advantage over the memoir in having been written at the time the events occurred. On 1 September 1785 Jefferson says, in a letter to Madison:

> I have received an application from the Directors of the public buildings to procure them a plan for their Capitol. I shall send them one taken from the best morsel of antient architecture now remaining. It has obtained the approbation of fifteen or sixteen centuries, and is therefore preferable to any design which might be newly contrived. It will give more room, be more convenient and cost less than the plan they sent me. Pray encourage them to wait for it, and to execute it. It will be superior in beauty to any thing in America, and not inferior to any thing in the world.[7]

On 20 September he wrote to Madison again:

> I received this summer a letter from Messrs. Buchanan and Hay as directors of the public buildings desiring I would have drawn for them plans of sundry buildings, and in the first place of a Capitol. They fixed for their receiving this plan a day which was within one month

of that on which their letter came to my hand. I engaged an Architect of capital abilities in this business. Much time was requisite, after the external form was agreed on, to make the internal distribution convenient for the three branches of government. This time was much lengthened by my avocations to other objects which I had no right to neglect. The plan however was settled. The gentlemen had sent me one which they had thought of. The one agreed on here is more convenient, more beautiful, gives more room and will not cost more than two thirds of what that would. We took for our model what is called the Maison-quarrée of Nismes, one of the most beautiful, if not the most beautiful and precious morsel of architecture left us by antiquity. It was built by Caius and Lucius Caesar and repaired by Louis XIV, and has the suffrage of all the judges of architecture who have seen it, as yielding to no one of the beautiful monuments of Greece, Rome, Palmyra and Balbec which late travellers have communicated to us. It is very simple, but it is noble beyond expression, and would have done honour to our country as presenting to travellers a morsel of taste in our infancy promising much for our maturer age. I have been much mortified with information which I received two days ago from Virginia that the first brick of the Capitol would be laid within a few days. But surely the delay of this piece of a summer would have been repaid by the savings in the plan preparing here, were we to value its other superiorities as nothing. But how is a taste in this beautiful art to be formed in our countrymen, unless we avail ourselves of every occasion when public buildings are to be erected, of presenting to them models for their study and imitation? Pray try if you can effect the stopping of this work. I have written also to E[dmund] R[andolph] on the subject. The loss will be only of the laying the bricks already laid, or a part of them. The bricks themselves will do again for the interior walls, and one side wall and one end wall may remain as they will answer equally well for our plan. This loss is not to be weighed against the saving of money which will arise, against the comfort of laying out the public money for something honourable, the satisfaction of seeing an object and proof of national good taste, and the regret and mortification of erecting a monument to our barbarism which will be loaded with execrations as long as it shall endure. The plans are in good forwardness and I hope will be ready within three or four weeks. They could not be stopped now but on paying their whole price which will be considerable. If the Undertakers are afraid to undo what they have done, encourage them to it by a recommendation from the assembly. You see I am an enthusiast on the subject of the arts. But it is an enthusiasm of which I am not ashamed, as its object is to improve the taste of my countrymen, to increase their reputation, to reconcile to them the respect of the world and procure them its praise.[8]

Jefferson's letter of the same date to Edmund Randolph contains a similar passage, with some omissions and slight changes of wording. In all of these statements, it will be seen, Jefferson says nothing unequivocal of any personal responsibility for the design, but writes, "I engaged an excellent architect to comply with [the commissioners'] desire," and emphasizes the merit of the model selected.[9]

One other published document bears on the question of authorship—the "Account of the Capitol in Virginia" published among Jefferson's miscellaneous papers. As numerous references to it will be necessary, it is reprinted here in full:

> The Capitol in the city of Richmond, in Virginia, is on the model of the Temples of Erectheus at Athens, of Balbec, and of the Maison quarrée of Nismes. All of which are nearly of the same form and proportions, and are considered as the most perfect examples of cubic architecture, as the Pantheon of Rome is of the spherical. Their dimensions not being sufficient for the purposes of the capitol, they were enlarged, but their proportions rigorously observed. The capitol is of brick, one hundred and thirty-four feet long, seventy feet wide, and forty-five feet high, exclusive of the basement. Twenty-eight feet of its length is occupied by a portico of the whole breadth of the house, showing six columns in front, and two inter-colonnations in flank. It is of a single order, which is Ionic; its columns four feet two inches diameter, and their entablature running round the whole building. The portico is crowned by a pediment, the height of which is two ninths of its span.
>
> Within the body of the building, which is one hundred and six feet long, are two tiers of rooms twenty-one feet high each. In the lower, at one end, is the room in which the Supreme Court sits, thirty feet by sixty-four feet with a vestibule fourteen feet by twenty-two feet, and an office for their clerk, fourteen feet by thirteen feet. In the other end is the room for the House of Delegates, thirty feet by sixty-four feet, with a lobby fourteen feet by thirty-six feet. In the middle is a room thirty-six feet square, of the whole height of the building, and receiving its light from above. In the centre of this room is a marble statute of General Washington, made at Paris, by Houdon, who came over to Virginia for the express purpose of taking his form. . . . A peristyle of columns in the same room, six feet from the wall, and twenty-two and a half feet high with their entablature, support a corridor above serving as a communication for all the upper apartments, the stairs landing in it. In the upper tier is a Senate chamber, thirty feet square, an office for their clerk, five rooms for committees and juries, an office for the clerk of the House of Delegates, a chamber for the Governor and Council, and a room for their clerk. In the basement of the building are the Land Office, Auditor's office, and Treasury.
>
> The drawings of the façade and other elevations, were done by Clarissault, one of the most correct architects of France, and author of the Antiquities of Nismes, among which was the Maison quarrée. The model in stucco was made under his direction, by an artist who had been employed many years in Greece, by the Count de Choiseul, ambassador of France at Constantinople, in making models of the most celebrated remains of ancient architecture in that country.[10]

The purpose and circumstances of the composition of this document, which would determine the weight to be accorded its statements, have been hitherto unknown. These points are cleared up, however, and fresh light is thrown on the main question by an exchange of letters between Jefferson and George Douglas, a bookseller and publisher of Petersburg, Virginia. On 15 October 1800, Douglas wrote to Jefferson concerning a proposed republication of *Douglas's Register* [*The Annual Register, and Virginia Repository*] for 1800. He said,

> to render it more acceptable to the people of Virginia, I propose to have a frontispiece to it representing a view of the Capitol in Richmond, the plate of which is now actually engraved in Philadelphia. . . . When in Richmond for the purpose of having the drawing taken, I endeavor'd, but in vain, to find some person who could give me an account of the building—the intention of this letter, therefore, is to request (having been informed, that you, Sir, were the original & principal mover in having the building undertaken and executed) that you will have the goodness to give me a short account of it—such as, from what original the design is taken, from Greece or Italy, of what order, the drawer or builder's names, when the work was commenced and when finished, and the expence, with some account of the inside apartments, etc.[11]

Jefferson replied from Washington on 21 December 1800:

> Your letter of Oct. 18 came to my hands on the 3d of Nov. when I was so engaged in preparations and arrangements for my departure to this place that I was only able to put up some notes on the subject of the Capitol that I had made when I gave the plan of it to Monsr. Clarissault. These have enabled me to make out the inclosed account of it. Whether the execution conformed to the original plan I do not know. Still less can I say anything of the expence: but that I presume might be obtained from Mr. William Hay who was one of the Directors, and principally attended to it.[12]

The description enclosed is substantially identical with the published "Account of the Capitol of Virginia," differing only in a few minor points of phrasing. The importance of Jefferson's accompanying letter lies partly in its explanation that his account described the original plan and not necessarily to the building as executed, but especially in its statement that he compiled his account from notes made when the plan was given to Clérisseau. The fullness of the description and dimensions suggests that the design had already been carried to an advanced state by Jefferson himself.

Of greater interest are the letters between Jefferson and the Directors of the Public Buildings of Virginia. The correspondence may be prefaced by the 1784 letter to Jefferson from William Short, afterward Jefferson's secretary in Paris, who shared his interest in architecture:

> The Assembly voted at their last session their Sale of the public Property here. In Order to begin the Buildings on the Hill the Directors have contracted with an Undertaker, and Ry[land] Randolph is to draw the Plan. I wished them very much to send to some Part of Italy for a Designer and Workmen. A good model I think would be of very great public Utility, and the Example of importing Workmen would unquestionably be followed and be attended

with very good Consequences. But I do not think the Directors believe it is possible to build a more magnificent House than the Wmsburg Capitol. It seems impossible to extend their Ideas of Architecture beyond it.[13]

Although Short thus appears as the original proponent of a design from abroad, his fears concerning the Directors were not realized, as we see from their first letter to Jefferson on 20 March 1785:

> The active part which you took before your departure from Virginia, as a director of the public buildings, leads us to believe, that it will not be now unacceptable to you, to co-operate with us, as far as your engagements will permit.
>
> We foresee, that in the execution of our commission, the Commonwealth must sustain a heavy expence, and that we can provide no shield so effectual against the censures which await large disbursements of public money, as the propriety of making them. For this purpose we must intreat you to Consult an able Architect on a plan fit for a Capitol, and to assist him with the information of which you are possessed.
>
> You will recollect, Sir, that the first act directed seperate houses for the accommodation of the different departments of government. But fearing that the Assembly would not countenance us in giving sufficient magnificence to distinct buildings, we obtained leave to consolidate the whole under one roof, if it should seem adviseable. The inclosed draught will show that we wish to avail ourselves of this licence, But, altho it contains many particulars it is not intended to confine the architect except as to the number and area of the rooms.
>
> We have not laid down the ground, it being fully in your power to describe it, when we inform You that the Hill on which Gunns yellow house stands and which you favoured as the best situation, continues to be preferd by us and that we have allocated 29 half acre lots, including Marsdon's tenement, and Minzies' lots in front of Gunns. The Legislature have not limited us to any sum; nor can we, as yet at least, resolve to limit ourselves to a precise amount. But we wish to unite oeconomy with elegance and dignity. At present the only funds submitted to our order are nearly about £10,000 Virga. Currency.
>
> We have already contracted with Edward Voss of Culpepper, for the laying of 1500 thousand Bricks. He is a workman of the first reputation here, but skilful in plain and rubbed work alone. We suppose he may commence his undertaking by the beginning of August. . . . This circumstance renders us anxious for expedition in fixing the plans, especially too as the foundation of the Capitol will silence the enimies of Richmond in the next October session. . . .
>
> We shall send to Europe for any Stone which may be wanted.
>
> The roof will be covered with lead, as we conceive that to be better than Copper or tiles.
>
> In the remarks, which accompany the plan, we have requested a draught for the Governor's house and prison. But we hope that the Capitol will be first drawn and forwarded to us, as there is no hurry for the other buildings.
>
> We trust Sir, you will excuse the trouble which we now impose on you, and will ascribe it to our belief of your alacrity to serve your Country on this occasion.[14]

Jefferson's immediate reply dated 15 June 1785 is lost, but subsequent letters from Paris permit us to recover its contents and to follow the later proceedings. In August he wrote:

Your favor of March 20 came to hand the 14th of June, and the next day I wrote to you acknowledging the receipt, and apprising you that between that date and the 1st of August it would be impossible to procure and get to your hands the draughts you desired. I did hope indeed to have had them prepared before this, but it will yet be some time before they will be in readiness. I flatter myself however they will give you satisfaction when you receive them and that you will think the object will not have lost by the delay. I was a considerable time before I could find an architect whose taste had been formed on a study of the antient models of this art: the style of architecture in this capital being far from chaste. I at length heard of one, to whom I immediately addressed myself, and who perfectly fulfills my wishes. He has studied 20 years in Rome, and has given proofs of his skill and taste by a publication of some antiquities of this country. You intimate that you should be willing to have a workman sent to you to superintend the execution of this work. Were I to send one on this errand from hence, he would consider himself as the Superintendant of the Directors themselves and probably of the Government of the state also. I will give you my ideas on this subject. The columns of the building and the external architraves of the doors and windows should be of stone. Whether these are made here, or there, you will need one good stone-cutter, and one will be enough because, under his direction, negroes who never saw a tool, will be able to prepare the work for him to finish. I will therefore send you such a one, in time to begin work in the spring. All the internal cornices and other ornaments not exposed to the weather will be much handsomer, cheaper and more durable in plaister than in wood. I will therefore employ a good workman in this way and send him to you. But he will have no employment till the house is covered, of course he need not be sent till next summer. I will take him on wages so long beforehand as that he may draw all the ornaments in detail, under the eye of the architect, which he will have to execute when he comes to you. It will be the cheapest way of getting them drawn and the most certain of putting him in possession of his precise duty. Plaister will not answer for your external cornice, and stone will be too dear. You will probably find yourselves obliged to be contented with wood. For this therefore, and for your window-sashes, doors, forms, wainscoating &c. you will need a capital housejoiner, and a capital one he ought to be, capable of directing all the circumstances in the construction of the walls which the execution of the plans will require. Such a workman cannot be got here. Nothing can be worse done than the house-joinery of Paris. Besides that his speaking the language perfectly would be essential. I think this character must be got from England. There are no workmen in wood in Europe comparable to those of England. I submit to you therefore the following proposition: to wit, I will get a correspondent in England to engage a workman of this kind. I will direct him to come here, which will cost five guineas. We will make proof of his execution. He shall also make himself, under the eye of the architect, all the drawings for the building which he is to execute himself: and if we find him sober and capable, he shall be forwarded to you. I expect that in the article of the drawings and the cheapness of passage from France you will save the expence of his coming here. But as to this workman I shall do nothing unless I receive your commands. With respect to your stone work, it may be got much cheaper here than in England. The stone of Paris is very white and beautiful, but it always remains soft, and suffers from the weather. The cliffs of the Seine from hence to Havre are all of stone. I am not yet informed whether it is all liable to the same objections. At Lyons and all along the Rhone is a stone as beautiful as that of Paris, soft when it comes out of the quarry, but very soon becoming hard in the open air, and very durable. I doubt how-ever whether the commerce between Virginia and Marseilles would afford opportunities of conveiance sufficient. It remains to be enquired what addition to the original cost would be made by the short land carriage from Lyons to the Loire and the water transportation down that to Bourdeaux, and also whether a stone of the same quality may not be found on the Loire. In this and all other matters relative to your charge you may command my services freely. . . . Will you have any occasion for slate? It may be got very good and ready prepared at Havre, and a workman or more might be sent on easy terms. Perhaps the quarry at Tuckahoe would leave you no other want than a workman.

I shall be glad to receive your sentiments on the several matters herein mentioned, that I may know how far you approve of them, as I shall with pleasure pursue strictly whatever you desire.[15]

In October 1785, James Buchanan and William Hay replied with gratitude for Jefferson's

undertaking in so obliging a manner to aid the Directors of the public buildings in procuring plans and estimates.

Your ideas upon the subject are perfectly corresponding to those of the Directors, respecting the stile and Ornaments proper for such a work, and we trust the plans will be designed in conformity thereto. We are sorry we did not sollicit your aid in the business at an earlier day, for, from the anxiety of the Public to have the work begun, we have been obliged to carry it on so far, that we may be embarrassed when we are favoured with a more perfect plan from you. As we expect to hear from you, and perhaps receive the plans before this can reach you, we deem it proper to inform you what has been done, that you may judge how far we shall be able to adopt the plan you transmit us. The foundation of the Capitol is laid, of the following demensions, 148 by 118 feet, in which are about 400,000 bricks; the Center of the building of 75 by 35 to be lighted from above, is designed for the Delegates; the rest is divided in such a manner as to answer every purpose directed by the Assembly; the foundation of the four porticos are not laid, tho' the end and side walls are contrived to receive them. The present plan differs from the One transmitted you, only in the arrangement, and we hope we shall be able to avail ourselves of your assistance with-out incurring much expence.[16]

Early in the new year, Jefferson wrote another detailed letter to the Directors.

I had the honour of writing to you on the receipt of your orders to procure draughts for the public buildings, and again on the 13th of August. In the execution of those orders two methods of proceeding presented themselves to my mind. The one was to leave to some architect to draw an external according to his fancy, in which way experience shews that about once in a thousand times a pleasing form is hit upon; the other was to take some model already devised and approved by the general suffrage of the world. I had no hesitation in deciding that the latter was best, nor after the decision was there any doubt what model to take. There is at Nismes in the South of France a building, called the Maison quarrée, erected in the time of the Caesars, and which is allowed without contradiction to be the most perfect and precious remain of antiquity in existence. Its superiority over any thing at Rome, in Greece, at Balbec or Palmyra is allowed on all hands; and this single object has placed Nismes in the general tour of travellers. Having not yet had leisure to visit it, I could only judge of it from drawings, and from the relation of numbers who had been to see it. I determined therefore to adopt this model, and to have all its proportions justly observed. As it was impossible for a foreign artist to know what number and sizes of apartments would suit the different corps of our government, nor how they should be connected with one another, I undertook to form that arrangement, and this being done, I committed them to an Architect (Monsieur Clérisseau) who had studied this art 20 years in Rome, who had particularly studied and measured the Maison quarrée of Nismes, and had published a book containing 4 most excellent plans, descriptions, and observations on it. He was too well acquainted with the merit of that building to find himself restrained by my injunctions not to depart from his model. In one instance only he persuaded me to admit of this. That was to make the Portico two columns deep only, instead of three as the original is. His reason was that this latter depth would too much darken the apartments. Oeconomy might be added as a second reason. I consented to it to satisfy him, and the plans are so drawn. I knew that it would still be easy to execute the building with a depth of three columns, and it is what I would certainly recommend. We know that the Maison quarrée has pleased universally for near 2000 years. By leaving out a column, the proportions will be changed and perhaps the effect may be injured more than is expected. What is good is often spoiled by trying to make it better.

The present is the first opportunity which has occurred of sending the plans. You will accordingly receive herewith the ground plan, the elevation of the front, and the elevation of the side. The architect having been much busied, and knowing that this was all which would be necessary in the beginning, has not yet finished the Sections of the building. They must go by some future occasion as well as the models of the front and side which are making in plaister of Paris. These were absolutely necessary for the guide of workmen not very expert in their art. It will add considerably to the expence, and I would not have incurred it but that I was sensible of its necessity. The price of

fig. 38 Maison Carrée, perspective, from *Antiquités de la France*, by Charles-Louis Clérisseau, 2d edition, 1804

the model will be 15 guineas. I shall know in a few days the cost of the drawings which probably will be the triple of the model; however this is but my conjecture. I will make it as small as possible, pay it, and render you an account in my next letter. You will find on examination that the body of this building covers an area but two fifths of that which is proposed and begun; of course it will take but about one half the bricks; and of course this circumstance will enlist all the workmen, and people of the art against the plan. Again the building begun is to have 4 porticos; this but one. It is true that this will be deeper than those were probably proposed, but even if it be made three columns deep, it will not take half the number of columns. The beauty of this is ensured by experience and by the suffrage of the whole world; the beauty of that is problematical, as is every drawing, however well it looks on paper, till it be actually executed; and tho I suppose there is more room in the plan begun, than in that now sent, yet there is enough in this for all the three branches of government and more than enough is not wanted. This contains 16 rooms, to wit, 4 on the first floor, for the General court, Delegates, Lobby, and Conference; eight on the 2d floor for the Executive, the Senate, and 6 rooms for committees and juries, and over 4 of these smaller rooms of the 2d floor are 4 Mezzanines or Entresoles, serving as offices for the clerks of the Executive, the Senate, the Delegates and the court in actual session. It will be an objection that the work is begun on the other plan. But the whole of this need not be taken to pieces, and of what shall be taken to pieces the bricks will do for inner *fig. 39* Thomas Jefferson's account with the commonwealth of Virginia, 9 December 1789. Jefferson reported his payments to Clérisseau for "his assistants in drawing the plans of Capitol" and to Fouquet for the model. The account also recorded Jefferson's purchase of a "coffee pot" as a gratuity to Clérisseau.

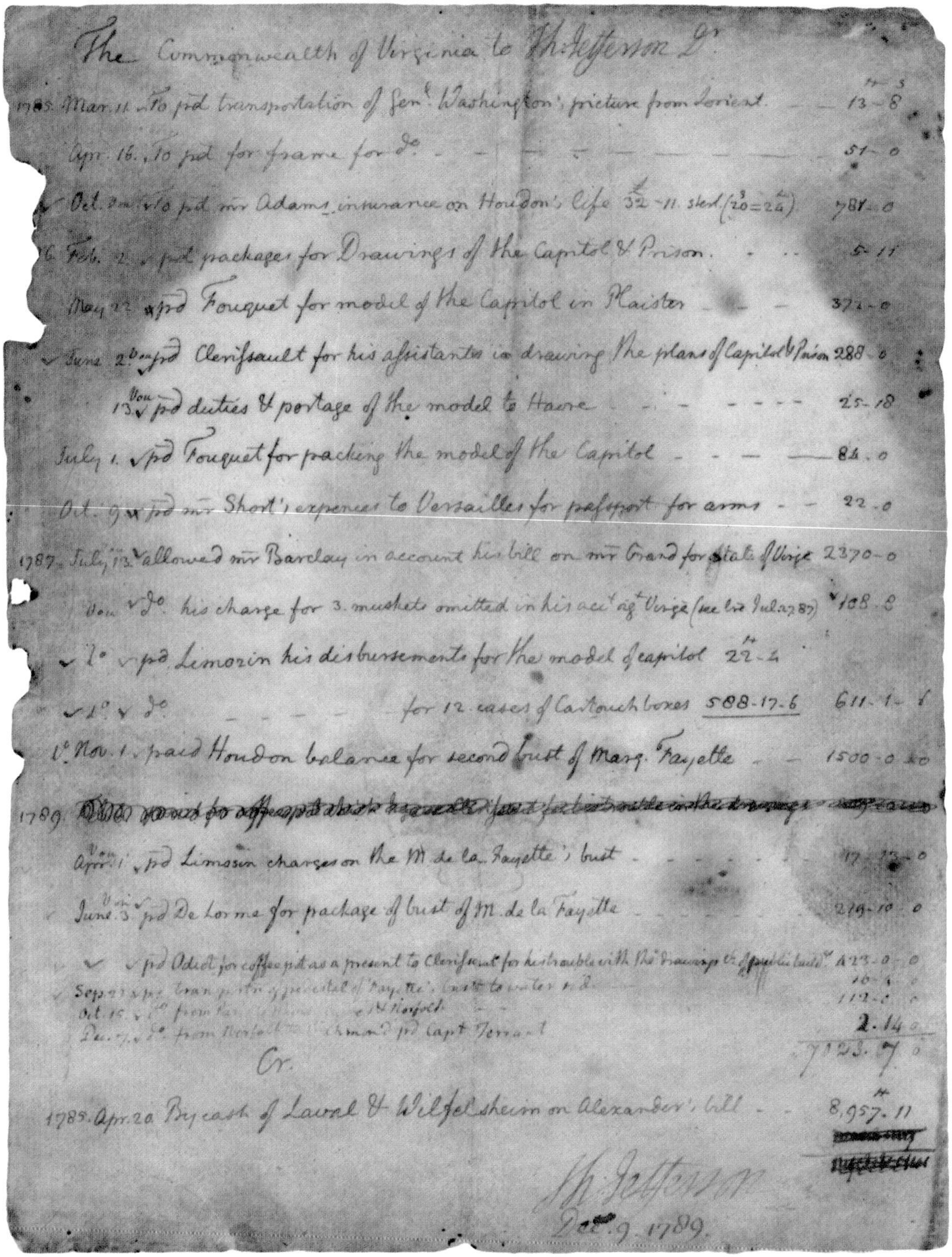

work. Mortar never becomes so hard and adhesive to the bricks in a few months but that it may easily be chipped off. And upon the whole the plan now sent will save a great proportion of the expence.

    . . . In my letter of Aug. 13. I mentioned that I could send workmen from hence. As I am in hopes of receiving your orders precisely in answer to that letter I shall defer actually engaging any till I receive them. In like manner I shall defer having plans drawn for a Governor's house &c. till further orders, only assuring you that the receiving and executing these orders will always give me a very great pleasure, and the more should I find that what I have done meets your approbation.[17]

On the following day, 27 January 1786, Jefferson wrote to James Monroe:

I send by this packet drawings for the Capitol and prison at Richmond. They are addressed to the Directors of the public buildings. If you have a curiosity to see them, open the round package which goes herewith, only being so good as to do them up again in the same way and send them off by the first post. I think they will be a gratification to yourself and such members as like things of that kind.[18]

The progress of the plaster model can be traced in subsequent letters. On 13 June 1786, Jefferson wrote from Paris to Buchanan and Hay, "The model of the Capitol being at length finished I have sent it down the Seine to Havre, it being necessary that it should go by water."[19] Finally, on 26 December, he explained a vexing delay and enclosed the bill of lading for the "Model of the Capitol, by which it appears that it has been shipped a few days ago."[20]

    The impression already given from Jefferson's memoirs that he himself dictated the style of the building, selected the precise model, and drew the plans of the interior, is greatly strengthened by these letters. Jefferson had expressed "ideas respecting the stile and Ornaments proper for such a work" immediately upon receipt of the first letter from the directors and devoted a "considerable time" finding "an architect whose taste had been formed on a study of the antient models of this art."[21] He not only decided on following the Maison Carrée before he went to Clérisseau, but he constantly resisted Clérisseau's suggestions to depart from the model in this or that respect. Jefferson's letters in which these statements occur are to be sure colored by his desire to secure the adoption of the design by invoking the authority of antiquity and the professional reputation of Clérisseau. For this reason, however, we may be confident that he does not overstate his own contribution, and we may conclude that he was responsible for at least as much as has just been outlined.[22]

    Evidence on the nature of Clérisseau's service is given by their accounts and correspondence in the archives. In Jefferson's account with the commonwealth of Virginia, dated 9 December 1789 (fig. 39), occurs the entry: "1786 June 2, Pd. Clerissault for his assistants in drawing the plans of Capitol &

Prison, 288 fr." The voucher accompanying this is an account in Clérisseau's handwriting (fig. 40), translated as follows:

Disbursement for Mr. Jefferson

the plans for the prison, section and elevation	2 Louis
the plans of the model, ground floor and first floor	2 Louis
the elevation of the facade	2 Louis
side elevation	2 Louis
the antiquities of Nîmes	3 Louis
all the measurements and sections	
for the execution of the model	1 Louis
	12 Louis

It must be noted that all the drawings had to be done twice before they were drawn properly. I do certify that the above Acc[oun]t Am[ou]nts to 288 Livres.

9dec89   Jh. LATIL[23]

Clérisseau's letter of acknowledgment bearing the same date, likewise speaks only of payment of expenses and makes it certain that he regarded the transaction, as Jefferson did, rather as a loan of his draftsmen for the drawing up of Jefferson's design than as regular professional services:

Sir,

I am touched by the kindness you showed in sending me my expenses. As for the obliging manner in which you expressed yourself, I am even more gratified by that. I am entirely pleased when I am certain that you are pleased with the zeal with which I seconded your intentions. Oh that I might be permitted to be greatly honored in finding some means by which to merit your confidence and your friendship. The love I have for my art is such that I cannot express to you how much I have been gratified to find a true lover of antiquity. I shall have the honor of seeing you to talk with you and prove to you that the pleasure I derived from obliging you was greater than my pains. I am, with all the consideration you deserve, Sir, your very humble, very obedient servant

CLÉRISSEAU

at Auteuil this 2 June 1786[24]

Two later letters from Clérisseau to Jefferson are preserved: one dated 16 March 1792 at the Massachusetts Historical Society, the other dated 23 May 1797 in the Library of Congress. They testify, however, merely to Clérisseau's confidence in Jefferson's friendliness. The first recommended a compatriot

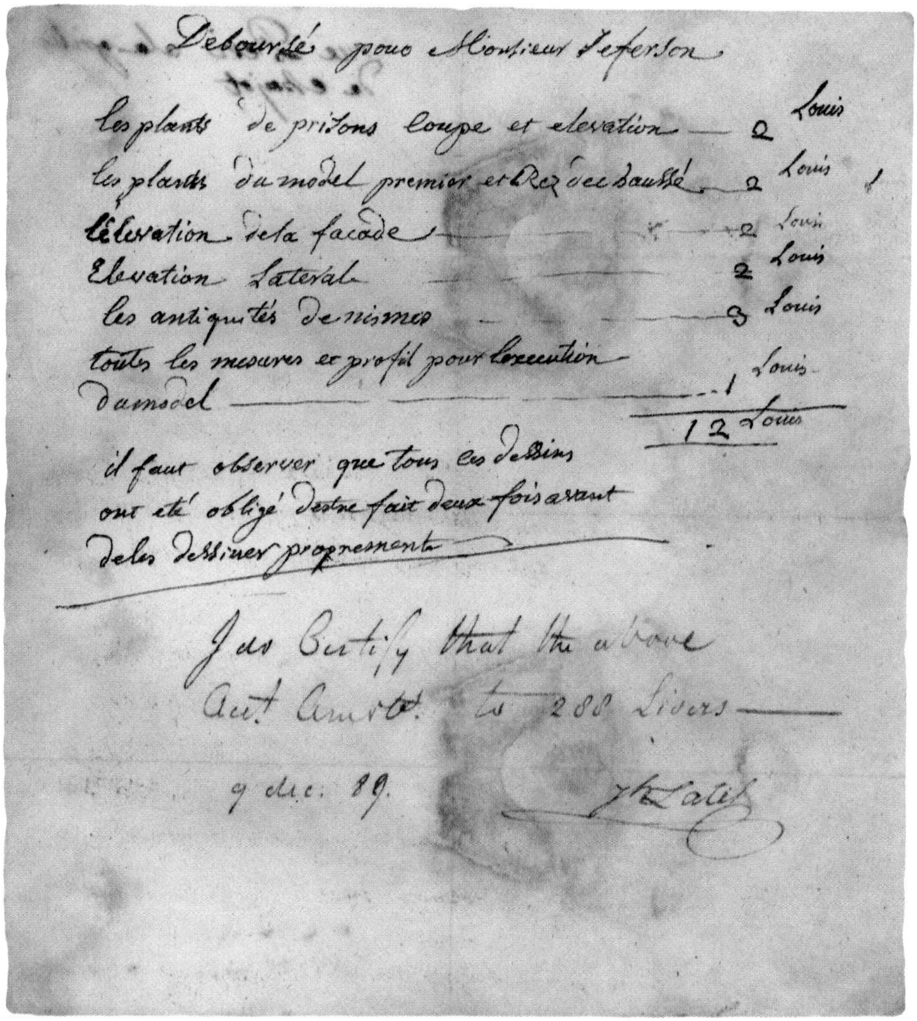
Debourse pour Monsieur Jefferson

les plants de prisons coupe et elevation — 2 Louis
les plants du model premier et Rez de chaussé — 2 Louis
lelevation dela facade — 2 Louis
Elevation lateral — 2 Louis
les antiquités de nismes — 3 Louis
toutes les mesures et profil pour lexecution du model — 1 Louis
12 Louis

il faut observer que tous ces dessins ont eté obligé destre fait deux fois avant deles dessiner proprement

I do Certify that the above Acct. Amots. to 288 Livres —

9 dec. 89.

fig. 40 Charles-Louis Clérisseau's account with Thomas Jefferson, 9 December 1789

who was immigrating to America; the second, written in poverty during the French Revolution, offered his library for sale. Among the polite formulas with which this second letter opened, he said:

> I still have the deepest feelings for a person who was so kind as to honor me with his confidence and who deigned to be pleased with my productions.[25]

As the productions referred to might well include Clérisseau's book, which Jefferson had bought, his drawings of antiquities, and other architectural works, no inference is to be drawn that Clérisseau was the designer of the Capitol. On the contrary, the written documents demonstrate that Jefferson's part was by far the larger than Clérisseau's—a fact that examination of the drawings confirms.

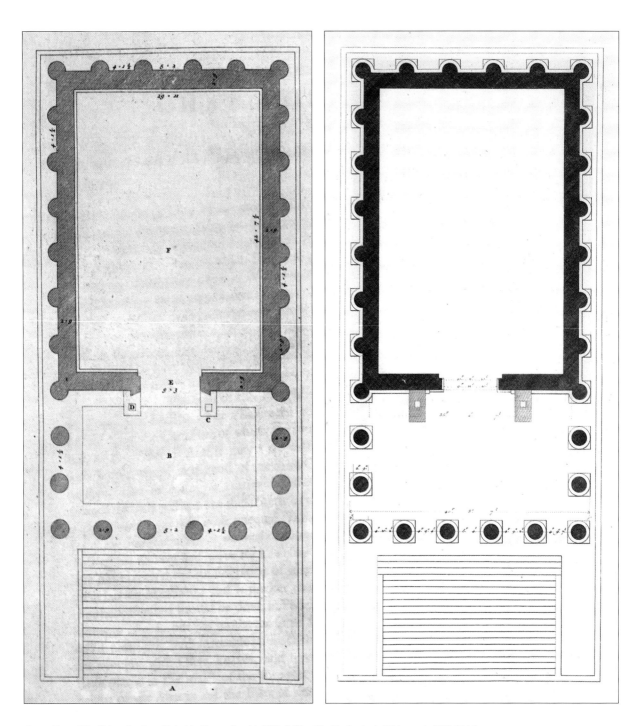

fig. 41 Plans of the Maison Carrée published by Giacomo Leoni in 1721 *(left)* and by Charles-Louis Clérisseau in 1778 *(right)*

The Original Design

A drawing preserved in the Coolidge Collection at the Massachusetts Historical Society in Boston is the "inclosed draught" sent to Jefferson on 20 March 1785 by the Directors of the Public Buildings (fig. 30). Their "remarks . . . which accompany the plan" have not survived, but this drawing is clearly the rough sketch by which James Buchanan and William Hay conveyed to Jefferson their idea of the commonwealth's needs. Their sketch shows a rectangular floor plan with a central hall traversing the building on each of two stories. The rooms arranged on either side of these hallways correspond in number and relative importance with those Jefferson described in his designs. Notations in the margins suggest that windows be placed as "found most convenient in the Ellivation" and that small porticoes be added at the ends and sides. Buchanan and Hay reported to Jefferson that in order to quell critics who wanted to move the seat of government out of Richmond, a rectangular foundation for the new Capitol was hastily laid prior to the October 1785 meeting of the General Assembly but that "the foundation of the four porticos are not laid, tho' the end and side walls are contrived to receive them." The evolution of Jefferson's design for the Capitol of Virginia begins with this modest sketch and can be traced through the subsequent drawings, in Jefferson's own hand, also preserved in the Coolidge Collection.[1]

Self-taught as a draftsman, and approaching architecture with geometric and formal preconceptions fostered by his allegiance to Andrea Palladio, Jefferson worked in a manner that was calculated, mechanical, and precise—the very antithesis to the free and intuitive method of men of artistic training, such as Clérisseau. The exactness and Palladian detail of the elevations of the Capitol repeat verbatim the language of corresponding drawings made by Jefferson before his European journey.

Before studying the design as exhibited in the final series of drawings it will be well to examine their possible sources on the formal side—the drawings of the Maison Carrée that were accessible to Jefferson. The building is figured in Book IV of Palladio's *Architecture of A. Palladio; In Four Books*, Jefferson's prime authority in previous years. It is shown with greater detail and exactness in Clérisseau's *Antiquités de la France: Monumens de Nîmes*, which Jefferson mentions in his memoir. We have seen that he purchased a copy from the author, charging it to the state; an entry, whether for this copy or another, appears in the catalog of his private library. Jefferson also acquired an additional copy of Palladio while in Paris,[2] but we do not know the dates of these purchases.

In Palladio's engraving the dimensions of the building are rationalized—altered—to conform to the modular system that the author, following Vitruvius, everywhere introduced. The lower diameter of the column being taken as a module, the height of the column and entablature are given as ten modules and as two and a half modules respectively, the intercolumniation as one and a half modules, or "pycnostyle"—the close spacing of Vitruvius. In Clérisseau's plates, on the other hand, all the dimensions, even those apparently corresponding to each other, are given minutely in French feet and inches. Frequently differing in absolute size from the measurements as stated by Palladio, they result in a somewhat different set of proportional ratios, less conveniently integral. Column and entablature, to be sure, are of nearly the same proportional height, but the space between the columns averages about one and three-fourths modules, instead of one and a half, a spacing justified by no classical theory. Since the number of columns and spaces are the same in each case, it follows that the total proportions of the length to the width vary substantially in Palladio's and Clérisseau's representations of the Maison Carrée. It should therefore be relatively easy—provided Jefferson did, in fact, rigorously observe the proportions—to see which authority he followed, and ascertain which study in the series, from its closer relations with the prototype, seems to have been made first.

There can be no question that Jefferson's first design derived from the engravings of Clérisseau's *Monumens de Nîmes*. The exterior of Plan 1 (fig. 34) is arranged (with a negligible percentage of error) exactly on the same proportions as in Clérisseau's plan. The scale, however, was much greater, the total length being 153 feet 9 inches, against about 85 English feet for the Maison Carrée. The module, or the diameter of the column, was 5 feet 5 inches, against about 3 feet. Neither of these important dimensions is in round numbers, and, one wonders, exactly what did determine the size? The answer would seem to be furnished by the striking coincidence between Jefferson's study and the Directors' sketch. If the depth of their porticoes is added to the scaled length of their main mass, the total length amounts to 153 feet 6 inches—identical with the total length of Jefferson's study. The exterior of Jefferson's first scheme, then, was determined by the proportions of the Maison Carrée as given by Clérisseau, and, very naturally, by the extreme dimension furnished by the Directors.

The interior disposition, in contrast with that shown by the Directors, is clear and corresponds in general with Jefferson's description and with the building as executed. A monumental square hall, rising through two stories and focusing on the pedestal for Washington's statue, occupies the center of the cella, or interior. The two principal rooms are at the ends and the shallow rooms, one containing the stairs, are at the sides. The precise relative sizes of these rooms were determined by the placement of the windows, two bays of the side serving each of the end rooms and three the central hall. This gave a large central space, permitting a peristyle of six columns each way, but made the end rooms comparatively narrow, twenty-five feet by seventy. Galleries supported on columns and railings subdividing these rooms do not noticeably improve this disproportion. The second story (fig. 35) has the same main divisions as the first, with a second order of columns in the central hall, and with smaller rooms separated by thin partitions over the long rooms at the ends. The various rooms in the first-floor plan were indicated by capital letters, referring to an accompanying legend that has not been found. The distribution of these letters is identical with that on later plans that permit a readier identification of the intended functions.

The two remaining designs, Plan 2 (fig. 32) and Plan 3 (fig. 31), show little or nothing outside the ashlar lines of the cella and obviously embody attempts to improve the proportions of the individual rooms. Each divides the length of the building into three equal parts, with a square central hall and end rooms twice the length of their breadth. Here the inspiration is evidently from a passage in Palladio's Book I: "In the length of halls I use not to exceed two squares, made from the breadth; but the nearer they come to a square, the more convenient and commendable they will be." Palladio thought that "the most beautiful and proportionable manner of rooms" had the dimensions of a square or of two squares.[3] The difficulty of these schemes, in which Jefferson determined the interior first, was that of afterwards fitting the exterior order to it. Neither of the schemes allowed the placement of either columns or pilasters along its sides, no matter what their proportions, and each had five spaces on the end and seven on the side, all equal, as in the original. Even had the spacing been different on the ends and sides, the new proportions of the interior would not have permitted a symmetrical position of the windows in the end rooms. These difficulties might have been overcome by the omission of the exterior order along the sides, as in the studies for the elevations, and may well have given Jefferson the first suggestion for the omission, although the possibilities of freedom thereby secured ultimately were not utilized in these drawings.

The interior arrangement of the first story is substantially identical in the two studies, but the second story, shown only in Plan 3, has a reduced central hall with four columns on a side in the first story and none in the second, a simple railing being substituted there. In one of the end rooms of the second drawing, however, the greater width was used to enhance the room with a basilican arrangement of columns leading up to the railed semicircular space, or exedra, at the end. The stairs were moved into the aisle of the central hall, but otherwise the arrangement, both upstairs and down, follows the general lines of the first study.

The basilican colonnade, just mentioned, now provides the clue to the arrangement of the rooms. The room with the letter *A* in the first study can denote nothing else but the courtroom, for which Palladio himself recommended and illustrated a form on the antique model in Book III, plate 17. *D* must then be the chamber of the House of Delegates. *F*, the central hall, must be the conference room, *E* the House lobby, *B* the vestibule to the courtroom, and *C* the office for its clerk. Upstairs, the Senate was certainly meant to have the large room with a gallery situated over one end of the courtroom. All this corresponds perfectly with the indications given by Jefferson in his "Account of the Capitol in Virginia" and in his letter of 26 January 1786 to the Directors of the Public Buildings.

The principal difference between Plan 2 and Plan 3—and a very notable one—lies in the intended relation of the porticoes to the central mass. In Plan 2, instead of the single deep portico, Jefferson suggested a portico at each end, only one bay deep—a radical departure from the prototype made either in the interest of formal symmetry or to express the balance of legislative and judicial functions. The external walls were left incomplete to permit adjustment of the fenestration, but the faces of the corner columns project so little beyond the outer face of the walls that only pilasters could have been intended, and they perhaps only at the corners. The diameter of the columns shown would result in an intercolumniation of about two and a half modules, against one and three-quarters for Clérisseau's Maison Carrée and Jefferson's first study. Intercolumniation of two and a quarter modules is associated with Palladio's Ionic order and Jefferson's studies for the elevations with Ionic columns. There can be little question, then, that the change from Corinthian to Ionic was already proposed when Plan 2 was made.

Plan 3 shows not even a vestige of colonnade, yet it may safely be assumed from the way Jefferson positioned the interior on the paper that a single deep portico was again intended at the bottom. That this drawing was made later than the others may now be proved. Plans 1 and 2 were made on one kind of engraved coordinate paper, while the elevations that embody the final design are on another kind, likewise engraved. Plan 3, however, was made on an improvised sheet imitating the style of the earlier engraved sheets. It must obviously have been made after Plans 1 and 2 but before the elevations.

Three elevations (figs. 33, 36–37) do not correspond exactly to any of the Plans, but show further changes of dimensions and proportions of the same sort as those between one Plan and the next. This may point to a certain interval between the dates of composition and possibly to the making of intermediate studies, now lost, but it must not be forgotten that Jefferson's mathematical methods made it possible to derive an elevation without drawing the corresponding plan. The difference of paper is not significant, for Jefferson had temporarily run out of red-lined paper before he made Plan 3.

The earlier of the elevations (fig. 33) shows the side of the building with a portico at each end, one bay deep, as in Plan 2. The Ionic order is of the conventional Palladian proportions, with a module, or column diameter, of 4 feet 2 inches. Again, as in Plan 2, pilasters occur only at the corners of the building and are moved away from the end windows in an effort to widen the rooms inside while keeping the windows symmetrical within the rooms. Jean-Pierre Fouquet's model and the finished building show that Jefferson considered the experiment with two porticoes unsuccessful. He then made the pair of drawings (figs. 36–37). Their equality of modules and heights proves that the front elevation here belonged with this side elevation rather than the earlier one. Although these drawings do not conform in every respect to the finished building, clearly they best represent the final design as Jefferson himself committed it to paper.

The scheme shown retains the single portico of the original, but this is two columns in depth instead of three, and the side wall is plain with but a single pilaster next to the portico. The building is laid out on a module of 4 feet 4 inches, with the column nine modules high, the entablature one and four-fifths, and the intercolumniation two and a quarter modules, all as recommended by Palladio. The total length of the building is almost exactly what would be obtained by figuring the length of a columnar building of the same number of bays and the same module. Near the corner the relation of the pilaster to the end window was not changed (as in the rejected study), and the window placement was such that pilasters might be added without any change (as they actually were added when the building was erected). The proportions of the end rooms, assuming that they were still based on the fenestration, were between the long-and-narrow form of Plan 1 and Palladio's ideal two-to-one ratio.

The forms of detail—doors, windows, cornice, and capitals—are all forms shown by Palladio that Jefferson had already used with equal literalness in his designs for Monticello. Certain problems met there for the first time, such as the Ionic capital on the angle and the return of the corner pilaster, are handled in a tentative and unsuccessful way, but in general the design is well studied and consistent. As in Jefferson's earlier work, the classical forms are still rationalized according to Palladian rules. The height of the pediment, for instance, is determined by Palladio's general formula—two-ninths of the span—instead of the proportions given for the Maison Carrée. Indeed we now see clearly that Jefferson's insistence on the exactness with which he had followed the Maison Carrée was largely to prevent further tampering with his design, which really departed from its model in almost every way—in dimensions, in proportion, in arrangement, and in detail. For the first time in Jefferson's architectural work, the whole effect was not merely Palladian. The temple form appears—the effect is Palladianized Roman.

The relation of these drawings to Jefferson's written descriptions of his design (for the Directors in 1786, for George Douglas in 1800, and for his memoir in 1821) now becomes evident. In composing the later descriptions Jefferson consulted not his drawings but rather notes, since lost, bearing calculations similar to those for Monticello that survive in his notebooks. Minor discrepancies in measurements given to Douglas and in the memoir can be attributed to the difficulty of recomputing the dimensions of the building from notes that were more than a decade old. Differences between Plan 1 and Jefferson's descriptions are greatest, but there can be no doubt that the elevations we have identified as the final studies (figs. 36–37) were given to Clérisseau. Jefferson's authorship of the design is thus given another confirmation.

That Clérisseau did make some positive contributions to the design, however, is also certain. Some of these appear in soft-pencil lines added with professional facility to Jefferson's laborious and precise elevations in the front view and the final side view (the rejected side view having none). The principal changes affect the frames of the doors and windows and the slope of the pediment. Consoles were added at the sides of the doors and beneath the windowsills, panels were introduced below the sills of the first-story windows and between the upper and lower ranges, and minor changes in the size and projection of the cornice members were indicated. The apex of the pediment was lowered so that its proportions, instead of being Jefferson's favorite 2:9, corresponded to the slope of the Maison Carrée as shown in Clérisseau's engraving. Pedestals were suggested to buttress the steps that were necessary to reach the side doors.

Minor differences between the plaster model and the Capitol building as executed caused doubts to be expressed in the nineteenth century as to whether or not the model was the original sent from France. In fact these very differences prove that the model could not have been made subsequently, for it exactly corresponds with Jefferson's drawings. As further evidence of its authenticity the original vouchers and instructions for unpacking the model (fig. 42) are preserved in the collections of the Virginia State Library. The model had been carefully packed for its trip across the Atlantic. Inside the exterior shipping crate, the plaster model was protected within a smaller box. "Be careful that the bottom of the small box is secured to the base of the model with six iron screws in order to render it immobile," the instructions advised.[4] The holes for these six screws still exist in the underside of the platform.

The model displayed today in the Capitol shows the essential design of Jefferson's final studies, with the modifications indicated upon them by Clérisseau. There are some further changes of relatively slight importance: the frieze and cornice of the second-story window caps are removed and small oblong windows are placed over them. The pediment of the side door is replaced by a horizontal cornice, the steps at the side are turned along the building, and the columns and pilasters are fluted. The actual dimensions of the model are, in general, exactly twice the corresponding dimensions of Jefferson's final studies—the scale of the model being five English feet to the English inch. Clérisseau made no changes in Jefferson's dimensions, further evidence for the conclusion that the Frenchman's role in the designs was secondary.

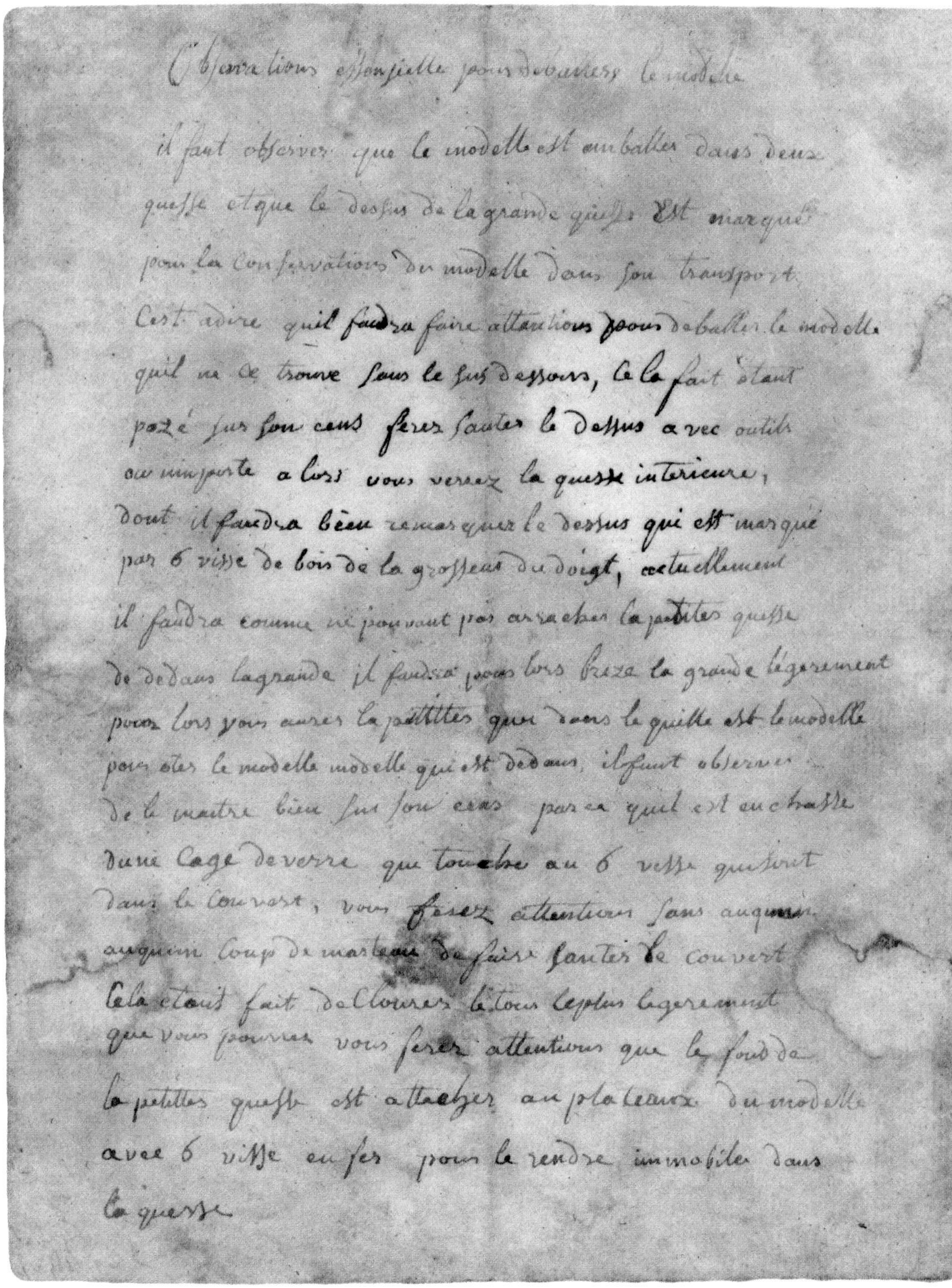

Observations essentielle pour deballer le modelle

il faut observer que le modelle est emballer dans deux
quisse et que le dessus de la grande quisse est marqué
pour la conservation du modelle dans son transport.
C'est adire qu'il faudra faire attention pour deballer le modelle
qu'il ne ce trouve sous le sus dessous, cela fait étant
pozé sur son cens ferez sauter le dessus avec outils
ou n'importe alors vous verrez la quisse intérieure,
dont il faudra bien remarquer le dessus qui est marqué
par 6 visse de bois de la grosseur du doigt, actuellement
il faudra comme né pouvant pas arracher la petites quisse
de dedans la grande il faudra pour lors breza la grande légèrement
pour lors vous aurez la petittes quen dans le quelle est le modelle
pour ôter le modelle modelle qui est dedans, il faut observer
de le maitre bien sur son cras parce qu'il est enchassé
dans cage de verre que touche au 6 visse qui sont
dans le couvert, vous ferez attention sans aucun
aucun coup de marteau de faire sauter le couvert
cela étant fait déclouver le tour le plus légèrement
que vous pourrez vous ferez attention que le fond de
la petittes quisse est attacher au plateaux du modelle
avec 6 visse en fer pour le rendre immobile dans
la quisse

fig. 42 "Observations essentielle," 1786. In his instructions for unpacking the fragile plaster of Paris model, Fouquet mentioned the "cage du verre," or glass cover, that would protect the model. The cover no longer survives, but Fouquet models in the collection of the Sir John Soane's Museum in London retain their original glass covers.

Clérisseau's Drawings of Jefferson's Design

The final drawings prepared by Clérisseau's draftsmen and sent to Virginia have not survived. The "ground plan, the elevation of the front, and the elevation of the side," which accompanied Jefferson's letter of 26 January 1786, arrived safely, as we know from their acknowledgment. The second-story plan was probably also included, as it appears with the others in Clérisseau's bill to Jefferson.[1]

The subsequent fate of these drawings is clear. On 11 July 1791, David Stuart, one of the commissioners for the new federal city on the Potomac, wrote to Governor Beverley Randolph, of Virginia, that Pierre Charles L'Enfant was

> drawing a model for the house of Legislature. I have mentioned to him the one sent in by Mr. Jefferson, which he desires to see. If there is no impropriety in it, I would beg you to send it to him by the stage. His residence is at Ge[orge] town. If not adopted, it shall be returned immediately.[2]

Two weeks later Governor Randolph replied that

> your Favour of the 11th instant was duly received and would have been immediately answered but for the absence of Mr. Hay one of the Directors of the public Buildings. I did not suppose that you expected the model of the Capitol in Plaister of Paris to be forwarded by the stage. I therefore called upon Mr. Hay for such drafts of the House as had been sent from France by Mr. Jefferson. You will receive inclosed in a small Tin case a Draft of the Ground plat together with a side and front View of the Building, which I beg may be returned as soon as Major L'Enfant can take copies of them as I am told they are essentially necessary for the completion of some work here.[3]

On 5 August Stuart again wrote:

> I have received your letter accompanied with the draft of the Public Buildings, and return you my thanks for your kindness. As soon as Major L'Enfant is done with it, I will return it.[4]

The promised return was never made, however, as we learn from a letter of 18 March 1799, written to Governor James Wood by William Hay, who was no longer serving as a Director of the Public Buildings:

> At the Time the late Beverly Randolph Esq. was Governour, the Plans and Drawings of the Capitol and the public Prison, which were sent from Paris by Mr. Jefferson, were delivered

to him & were by him transmitted in a Tin Case to the Directors of the public Buildings in the federal City. Since that Time I have never seen them.[5]

The reason for this is clear. L'Enfant was dismissed from the government service in February 1792—about six months after the time Virginia's Capitol drawings were entrusted to him—leaving the custody of his papers in dispute. The federal commissioners claimed that he declined to pass over the papers of his office; he protested that they were stolen by order of the commissioners during his absence.[6]

Fortunately the absence of the final drawings of the Virginia Capitol makes no serious gap in our information. There is no reason to question their exact correspondence to the plaster model Fouquet prepared from them. If the model had been corrected from the drawings in any important respect, Jefferson undoubtedly would have called attention to it, as he did to his desire for a deeper portico.

More to be regretted is the absence of the discarded set of drawings referred to by Clérisseau in his bill to Jefferson (fig. 40, p.17), which says "that all the drawings had to be done twice before they were drawn properly."[7] These might throw further light on the development of the design and on the relative contributions of Jefferson and Clérisseau, but

fig. 43 Charles-Louis Clérisseau, attributed to J. Fischer, ca. 1770

so far they have not been located. Catherine II of Russia bought and deposited in the Winter Palace (now the Hermitage Museum in Saint Petersburg) twenty volumes of Clérisseau's Roman architectural drawings. If these were purchased during Clérisseau's stay in Russia in 1778–1782 they cannot, of course, include the drawings of which we are in search. It is possible, however, that the purchase was made or supplemented in 1797 when, as we have seen, Clérisseau sought to dispose of his library.[8]

The necessity for a complete redrawing while the matter was in Clérisseau's hands is difficult to explain if Clérisseau's assistants had in hand from the start Jefferson's final studies with which the model agrees. It might imply merely that Jefferson changed his own ideas, or it might be thought to indicate that some of the changes that we have traced in the course of his studies resulted themselves from suggestions from Clérisseau, prior to those indicated on the elevations. While these questions cannot be decided with certainty, a number of not wholly consistent statements may be brought to bear upon them.

In his letter to George Douglas, Jefferson stated that his description was being written in December 1800 from notes made when he gave the plan to Clérisseau, yet the dimensions given in it correspond so closely with those of the final elevations as to make it improbable that a complete redrawing was undertaken for such minor changes.[9] The notes, however, may equally well have been made if Jefferson gave Clérisseau a second, revised plan.

Jefferson said in his letter of 26 January 1786 that it was Clérisseau who suggested that the portico be made only two columns deep, yet this arrangement appeared already in Jefferson's final side elevation. He said, however, that this was the only instance in which Clérisseau had persuaded him to depart from the prototype.[10] Numerous others remain, some of which at least seem more consonant with French methods of thought than with Jeffersonian methods. The complete omission of an engaged order, while it had ample precedent in other classical temples and might have resulted solely from economy, suggests the puristic ideas of the eighteenth century. This appears above all in the rejected side elevation with its shallow porticoes at both ends—so much better than the single deep portico for the expression of two rooms of equal importance, yet so contrary to Jefferson's declarations concerning the dangers of departure from the antique precedent.

Possibly a clue may be found in certain passages hitherto unstressed. Jefferson's memoir says: "I applied to M. Clerissault . . . to have me a model of the building made in stucco, only changing the order from Corinthian to Ionic."[11] Clérisseau's bill refers to two sets of plans for the building. It seems likely that the first was a close approximation of the Maison Carrée, undoubtedly with engaged columns and windows between as in Jefferson's earliest plan. After a set of drawings along these lines was begun under Clérisseau's direction, however, Jefferson no doubt discussed the matter with Clérisseau and incorporated his criticisms and suggestions along with fresh ideas of his own in the later plans and the elevations that became necessary as a result. He apparently decided not to use the two-portico scheme, but substituted the other modified study for the scheme already under way, and then made the notes on which the description sent to Douglas was based. Finally, giving these drawings to Clérisseau, who revised their detail but had his assistants draw them up otherwise unchanged, Jefferson at last received the final drawings he sent to Virginia.

The growth of the design and the responsibility for it should now be fairly clear. Jefferson's statements in his memoir are substantially accurate but understate his own part. His letters, though doing better justice to his share, purposely exaggerate the responsibility of Clérisseau and the imitation of the antique. In the letters to Madison and Randolph this is easily explained as due to delicacy in claiming credit for a design whose adoption he was urging on grounds of superior merit. In the letters to the Directors he emphasized Clérisseau's involvement to prevent departures from the scheme. The drawings and the model show that the design, though a classic adaptation developed with some criticism, was essentially Jefferson's own. The idea of such an adaptation was itself his, the Directors' sketch gave only the practical requirements and a limiting dimension. Clérisseau's attempts to rationalize the plan show that he can scarcely have suggested the literal imitation of the temple form. Jefferson not merely selected a model for the exterior and determined the arrangement of the interior, but he fixed every principal dimension, both inside and out, after elaborate study and the rejection of many alternatives—the final result having nothing in common with its prototype except the general form. The Ionic order, with the changed proportions that its adoption necessitated, was apparently Jefferson's idea. The omission of the order along the sides of the building may or may not have resulted from a suggestion by Clérisseau, but the new fenestration was Jefferson's. To Clérisseau are due, besides the reduced depth of the portico, certain minor changes and the final forms of details that influence stylistic aspects of the building, but not its mass, subdivision, proportions, or interior arrangement. If one man is to be designated as the architect of the Capitol of Virginia, it must unquestionably be Thomas Jefferson.

Jefferson's plan was boldly and logically conceived, with the principal rooms occupying the axial positions and the minor elements well subordinated. The major balance was not between the two branches of the legislature, as in the typical capitol of today, but between the judicial branch and the legislative, as represented by the House of Delegates. Perhaps the democratic tendencies of Jefferson account for this identification of the legislature with its popular house, for in practice the court scarcely needed a larger room than the Senate. The conference room, as the central hall was called, corresponded with the Virginia Constitution of 1776, which provided that the ballots cast "in each House respectively" for governor were to be "deposited [and examined]" in the Conference room.[12]

The exterior is an interesting compound of classicism and French academicism. The consoles and garlanded panels of the walls recall rather the manner of Jacques Ange Gabriel than of Palladio, as suggested by the earlier studies. The absence of pilasters along the sides conformed to classical and French structural purism, although it weakened the unity of the portico and walls. The exterior has the sleekness and accomplishment of eighteenth-century France, with nothing of the unstudied artlessness of colonial America. It possesses a grandiose classical quality—still relatively novel abroad—admirably symbolizing the aspirations of the new republican state. The glaring defects in the relation of the portico to the walls resulted from the antithesis that lay in the very program. As in the Roman triumphal arch and in Claude Perrault's colonnade of the Louvre, it was the civilization and majesty of the state that were to be symbolized, and the columns were used not only as elements of intrinsic magnificence but also as trophies of the classical culture of the builders. The portico was a frontispiece to all Virginia.

"Finished with the Proper Ornaments"

The Capitol building as executed did not conform entirely to the design sent from abroad. Thomas Jefferson's attempt to furnish his country with a perfect example of classical architecture was frustrated in part. He spoke in his memoir, as we have seen, of "some variations, not for the better, the most important of which, however, admit of future correction."[1] Much the same phrases occur, amid the pardonable expressions of triumph, in his letter to William Short upon first seeing the building after his return to America:

> Our new Capitol, when the corrections are made of which is susceptible, will be an edifice of first rate dignity. Whenever it shall be finished with the proper ornaments belonging to it (which will not be in this age) it will be worthy of being exhibited along side the most celebrated remains of antiquity.[2]

Jefferson's plans differed from the Capitol in ways that become apparent when we compare the evidence for the original form with the subsequent history of the building itself.

The early views of the Capitol were taken from such a distance or drawn at such small scale that they furnish little detailed information. The earliest extant depictions of the building, in four watercolor sketches of Richmond made between April 1796 and May 1798 by the architect Benjamin Henry Latrobe, show the main lines of the building essentially as they remained until 1904–1906, with pedimented roof and pilasters along the side walls.

The drawing mentioned by George Douglas in his October 1800 letter to Jefferson may not have been published immediately for the reasons explained in his subsequent letter, written in August 1801:

> Agreeable to my plan, I had a drawing or front elevation of the Capitol taken by a person in Richmond, and I got it engraved by one of the most eminent Artists in Philadelphia. The work was completed in the month of Dec. and I had every reason to expect the copies or impressions, here in January. After waiting two months for them, in March they sent me the plate itself, but the copies, by some unlucky accident or other, were lost or mislaid, and have not yet been found.[3]

Although Douglas's engraved plate arrived from Philadelphia too late for use in his almanac for 1801, he seems to have used it for the frontispiece for *The Virginia and North Carolina Almanack for the Year 1802*, published in Petersburg by Douglas and Ross in 1801. Although not familiar to the author in 1915, this frontispiece is now recognized as the earliest published view of the Capitol of Virginia (fig. 24, p. xxvii). From the inscriptions beneath the published image—"Sully, del[ineavit]" and "Lawson, sculp[sit]"—it seems clear

fig. 44 "View of the Capitol, Richmond, from Dr. James Macclurg's Dining room," by B. Henry Latrobe, 1797. Latrobe documented the Capitol's unfinished appearance atop Shockoe Hill. The facades, still of red brick with areas of whitewash, lacked their window frames, their coats of stucco, and their Ionic capitals, which were not put into place until late in 1797.

that Douglas's artist in Richmond was the miniaturist Lawrence Sully, elder brother of Thomas Sully, and that his engraver in Philadelphia was Alexander Lawson.[4]

Further particulars relating to the building are given by the descriptions of early travelers. The duc de La Rochefoucauld-Liancourt, an accurate and cultivated observer, gave this account of the Capitol in 1796:

> This edifice, which is extremely vast, is constructed on the plan of the "Maison Quarrée" at Nismes, but on a much more extensive scale. The attics of the Maison Quarrée have undergone an alteration in the Capitol, to suit them for the convenience of the public offices of every denomination, which, thus perfectly secure against all accidents from fire, lie within reach of the tribunals, the executive council, the governor, the general assembly, who all sit in the Capitol, and draw to it a great afflux of people. This building which is entirely of brick,

is not yet coated with plaster: the columns, the pilasters, are destitute of bases and capitals: but the interior and exterior cornices are finished, and are well executed. The rest will be completed with more or less speed: but, even in its present unfinished state, this building is, beyond comparison, the finest, the most noble, and the greatest in all America. The internal distribution of the parts is extremely well adapted to the purposes for which it is destined. It was Mr. Jefferson who, during his embassy in France, sent the model of it. Already it is said to have cost a hundred and seventy thousand dollars; and fifteen thousand more are the estimated sum requisite for completing it and remedying some defects which have been observed in the construction.[5]

In the same year, Isaac Weld, a critic less sympathetic as well as less competent, made this comment on the Capitol:

> From the opposite side of the river this building appears extremely well, as its defects cannot be observed at that distance, but on a closer inspection it proves to be a clumsy ill-shapen pile. The original plan was sent over from France by Mr. Jefferson, and had great merit; but his ingenious countrymen thought they could improve it, and to do so placed what was intended for the attic story, in the plan, at the bottom, and put the columns on the top of it. In many other respects, likewise, the plan was inverted. This building is finished entirely with red brick; even the columns themselves are formed of brick: but to make them appear like stone, they have been partially whitened with common whitewash. The inside of the building is but very little better than its exterior part. The principal room is for the house of representatives; this is used also for divine service, as there is no such thing as a church in the town. The vestibule is circular, and very dark. . . . Ugly and ill-contrived as this building is, a stranger must not attempt to find fault with any part of it, for it is looked upon by the inhabitants as a most elegant fabric.[6]

Obviously in his remark on the inversion of the attic story Weld merely revealed his own ignorance of the classical podium and unconsciously showed how much superior was Jefferson's knowledge of ancient architecture to the current tradition of the day.

The description of Karl Bernhard, duke of Saxe-Weimar-Eisenach, who visited Richmond in 1825, was more intelligent, but careless in some respects. He said of the Capitol:

> On the hill which commands the city, stands the state-house, called the capitol, surrounded by a newly laid out garden; it reminds one of the *Maison Quarrée* at Nismes in France. On one of the smaller sides of the parallelogram there is a portico of eight Ionic columns. But these columns are of wood only, and have, when closely inspected, a rather decayed appearance. On the two long sides, the building has two entrances with steps.[7]

Samuel Mordecai, an old resident of Richmond who published in 1856 his reminiscences of early days, said,

> The *Capitol* itself, not then stuccoed, exposed its bare brick walls between the columns or pilasters. The roof was once flat, if I mistake not, and paved with tiles, and, like Noah's Ark, "was pitched without, with pitch." But as a hot sun caused the pitch to flow down the gutters, and the rains to enter the halls, an elevated roof was substituted. In process of time, the attic thus formed was converted into an arsenal. The building and the fire-arms being perhaps considered fire-proof, or the risk not considered at all.[8]

More precise and reliable, although fragmentary, are the indications furnished by the official letters, accounts, and vouchers preserved at Richmond in the Virginia State Library.[9] The same is true of the later evidences, of which the most important are a set of geometrical drawings signed "Alb[ert] Lybrock, arch't and supt." and dated 1858. They comprise two parallel series, one showing the building as it then existed (figs. 47–49), and the other as it would be if remodeled by the addition of one bay at the rear and by certain minor changes. Only the first series is of interest, as this remodeling was never carried out. The series includes plans of each floor, front and side elevations, and sections, all of which are of the greatest accuracy in almost every point where they can still be verified.[10]

Photographs taken before the remodeling of 1904–1906 are another important supplementary source. They give the best idea of the interior detail and cover many points not shown by the drawings. What neither drawings nor photographs show in many cases, however, are the materials used in the different parts and the evidences of changes prior to 1858 that may lie concealed in various parts of the building.

The "Report of the Committee on the Enlargement, Restoration and Repair of the Capitol Building," far from clearing up these points, as it might well have done, does not even give a summary of the alterations made in the old building in 1904–1906.[11] There is likewise no itemization of the large sums expended by the contract (a listing that might have indicated exactly what the changes were) although certain incidental mentions and items for extra work in the accounts reveal a few of them. To supplement the bareness of the legislative report, the author sought from William C. Noland and Henry E. Baskervill, the Richmond architects among those associated in charge of the remodeling, the benefit of their knowledge of the building before its transformation and of their exceptional opportunities for observation during the reconstruction. In general their surveys and written memoranda made at the time were not preserved,[12] but their memories were clear on many points of interest.

Before the arrival of the final plans of the Capitol from France, considerable progress, as we have seen, had already been made on the building. The cornerstone was laid 18 August 1785, and two months later the Directors had written: "The foundation of the Capitol is laid, of the following demensions, 148 by 118 feet." Their further statement—"The present plan differs from the One transmitted you, only in the

Above: *fig. 45* "View of the City of Richmond from the Bank of the James River," by B. Henry Latrobe, 1798. In this last depiction of the Capitol, Latrobe showed the building's prospect as Jefferson intended. Set high on the hill, it was the focal point of the view. Early visitors likened it to the Temple of Poseidon at Sounion in Greece.

Left: *fig. 46* "View of Richmond from Bushrod Washington's Island," by B. Henry Latrobe, [1796], the earliest of four drawings in which Latrobe recorded the Capitol of Virginia. The artist captured this dramatic view of the new Capitol rising above its natural landscape from his vantage point on what is now called Belle Isle.

arrangement"—is obviously incorrect, as the draft sent to Jefferson shows the body of the building about 120 by 96 feet, a discrepancy they later admitted.[13]

Jefferson's plan differed from both; he knew difficulty was bound to arise over its adoption as his letters to Madison and Randolph have attested. He even wrote a second letter to Madison of the same tenor as the one already quoted.[14] Madison replied to the first that it had not arrived until 24 February 1786, too late for legislative action with regard to the Capitol. A letter from Attorney General Edmund Randolph, Madison continued,

> takes notice of the plan you had promised and makes no doubt that it will arrive in time for the purpose of the Commissioners. I do not gather from his expressions however that he was aware of the change, which will become necessary in the foundation already laid; a change which will not be submitted to without reluctance for two reasons. 1. The appearance of caprice to which it may expose the Commissioners. 2. Which is the material one, the danger of retarding the work till the next Session of Assembly can interpose a vote for its suspension, and possibly for a removal to Williamsburg. This danger is not altogether imaginary. Not a Session has passed since I became a member without one or other or both of these attempts. At the late Session, a suspension was moved by the Williamsburg Interest, which was within a few votes of being agreed to. It is a great object therefore with the Richmond Interest to get the building so far advanced before the fall as to put an end to such experiments. . . . The substitution of a more oeconomical plan, may better reconcile the Assembly to a prosecution of the undertaking.[15]

The outcome of the difficulty on the arrival of the plans, with the essential adoption of Jefferson's design, appears in the following letter 12 July 1786 to Jefferson from Edmund Randolph, then one of the Directors:

> Your favor concerning the capitol came to hand; after the most painful anxiety at the tardy movement of the plan to Virginia. We are at length relieved by its arrival. A council of directors was immediately called, and with some difficulty the plan was carried thro! But I am exceedingly afraid that we have committed some blunder even now. I directed Mr. Dobie, our superintendant, and an adept in draughtmanship, to furnish me with a narrative of our proceedings in technical language. When completed, it shall be forwarded. At present, however, I will give you some imperfect idea of it. The plan sent to you was a mere assay; that adopted by us was very different. When your plan was examined, it was conceived, that without adhering to precisely the same front, it would be enough to follow the same proportions. By this doctrine we were rescued from a great embarrassment, for the lowland interest and a strong party of the upland, in the assembly, are labouring to stop the progress of the building. To pull up all that had been done, would have been to strengthen the opposition. We have therefore resolved to pursue your plan in every respect, except the extension of the front. By this means we have been obliged to remove only one side wall and a few partition walls.[16]

The arrival of the model and its relation to the progress of the work are chronicled in a letter from William Hay to Jefferson, dated 3 May 1787:

> Your favour of the 26th December inclosing Bill of Lading for the Model of the Capitol came safe to hand, addressed to Mr. Buchanan and myself, and have to appologize for answering it in my private Capacity. There has not been a Meeting of the Directors of the Public Buildings for some considerable Time past and Mr. Buchanan is now confined by a severe spell of Sickness, so that I could neither have the Advice of the Directors nor the Assistance of Mr. Buchanan in the Business. No Delay in the work has been occasioned by the Models not coming to hand, last Summer, and I fear it will stop where it is now for some Time. The pedestal Basement and the principal story were finished by last October, and nothing has been done since. The fund of the 2 p[ercen]t. Additional Duties upon which was charged £5000 to be applied towards completing the public Buildings, has proved unproductive, for the Treasurer assures me, it will not produce the sum which was charged on it in the first Instance for the support of the Members of Congress. The Directors therefore can make no Contract upon this Fund without sacrificing too much to the extravagance of the Times, and when the Assembly meets again I fear no further Assistance will be given on account of the Distress which is universally complained of thro' the State. The Capitol may then remain in its present state for many Years. The Directors themselves have been neglectful, in many things and in none more, than in the want of Acknowledgements to you, for the great Assistance you have given them in this Business. Permit me therefore, to return my sincere thanks, and I am sure they will be those of the Directors in general, for the Interest you have taken in procuring proper Plans and a model for the Ornamenting the Capital of your native Country.[17]

The further progress of the building may be traced indirectly through the great mass of accounts and vouchers preserved at Richmond in the Virginia State Library. For our purposes, only the most important need be cited, those marking the principal stages or having references to changes from the design. The report of "a Committee to whom was referred the letter of the Directors of the public Buildings," dated 14 December 1789, found it "absolutely necessary for the preservation of the building from ruin that . . . there be immediately a pediment roof put on it to be covered with Lead." Samuel Dobie had contracted with the Directors in February 1787 "to put on the Capitol a flat roof which should be tight and durable," and Dobie worked hard to fulfill the contract, but by the end of 1789 it was "apprehended that it will be impracticable to make the roof a tight one."[18] Payments were authorized for this pedimented roof on 13 April and 11 November 1790.

The building of the portico is described in a letter from William Hay to Governor Beverley Randolph on 22 June 1790, stating that on 11 May 1789, "Edward Voss contracted with the Directors to build the Columns of the Portico, and the vault under the Portico, of Brick." Voss finished the columns late in the season of 1789, however, and "the Directors postponed the vaults until this season." In 1790 when Voss asked "for Permission

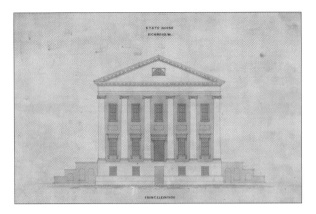

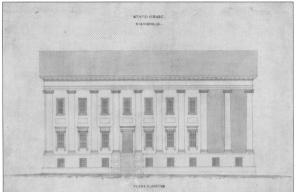

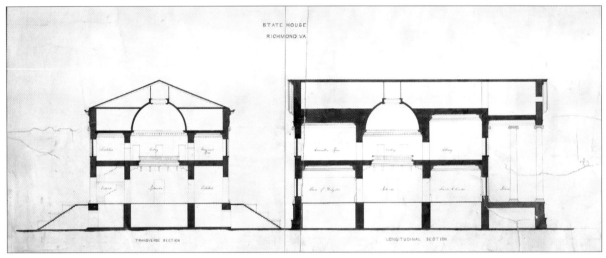

Clockwise from top left: *fig. 47* State Capitol, front elevation, by Albert Lybrock, 1858. The front elevation reveals the stairways at the sides of the building and the governor's office above the east vestibule; *fig. 48* State Capitol, flank elevation, by Albert Lybrock, 1858. Lybrock's carefully measured elevations and sections are an invaluable record of the structure of the Capitol before the Civil War. The first exterior stairs to the Capitol's side entrances, built in 1793 probably by Samuel Dobie, were replaced about 1818 and again in 1846 by the stairs shown in Lybrock's drawings; *fig. 49* State Capitol, transverse and longitudinal sections, by Albert Lybrock, 1858. The first floor of Lybrock's longitudinal section shows the House of Delegates chamber and gallery to the north, the rotunda in the center, and the Senate chamber near the portico; the second floor displays committee rooms to the north, the rotunda gallery and skylight, and the library above the Senate.

& Direction to begin the Vaults, the Directors excepted against the Columns as being, in their opinion insufficient . . . as it would be unsafe to trust a Lead cover of the Roof of the Portico until the columns are made sufficient." The Directors were "of the opinion that the Roof of the Portico should be shingled & the front & sides of the Pediment sheeted with Plank in order to preserve the Timbers from Injury."[19] Voss failed to take down and reerect the columns, however, and they were finally allowed to stand as they were. On 8 May 1792 the Directors resolved "that Dabney Minor be directed to whitewash the Pedestals upon the Top of the Capitol, & the Pilasters with Stone Lime with a mixture of Lamp black to give it the Resemblance of Stone," and on 14 June they wrote the governor, "Mr. Minor will soon furnish the Entablature."[20]

Not until 1797 was there an appropriation for completing the exterior, which had remained, meanwhile, as La Rochefoucauld-Liancourt saw it, without stucco or capitals. Then began a series of payments, the last of which, marking the completion of the building, was attested to the governor by William Foushee, one of the Directors, on 23 October 1798:

> Mr. Henry Robertson the undertaker to finish the outside of the Capitol, having nearly laid on all the coating, &c. I am also desired to request a warrant for One thousand Dollars under the appropriation of the last General Assembly for this purpose.[21]

The later history of the building includes no important changes before the proposed enlargement in 1858. The only interesting modification recorded is the opening of the window in the pediment for additional light in the garret in 1801.[22] As Lybrock's proposal for enlargement was not followed, the original fabric still remained substantially intact until 27 April 1870. On that day a catastrophe occurred. In the heated political atmosphere of Reconstruction, crowds gathered in the Capitol to witness the decision by the Virginia Supreme Court of Appeals on a case stemming from Richmond's violently contested mayoral election.

When the courtroom galley gave way under the weight, the second-story court chamber collapsed into the hall of the House of Delegates below. Sixty persons were killed and several hundred were injured.[23] In the aftermath of this tragedy, "resolutions were offered to pull down the Capitol and build a new one, but it was finally decided to repair the old building."[24] Photographs made after these repairs, by their substantial agreement with Lybrock's drawings of 1858, show that the architectural features of the House of Delegates (which had been crushed and gutted by the falling debris) were reconstructed with few changes from the previous design.

On 1 August 1904, after prolonged agitation and discussion, the building was turned over to contractors for enlargement. The remodeling was completed in the course of 1905, and the building was reoccupied in January 1906. The architects entrusted with the work were John Kevan Peebles, of Norfolk; Edward G. Frye and Aubrey Chesterman, of Lynchburg; and William C. Noland and Henry C. Baskervill, of Richmond. The scheme adopted by the legislature involved the construction of separate wings of lesser height for the House and Senate, connected with the original building by corridors at the old side doors, and the cutting up of the old House and Senate chambers for offices. A part of the original material was replaced by new. Although they apparently ignored the plaster model, the architects tried to revert to Roman forms and the proportions of the Maison Carrée in matters of form and detail where these had been lost by the builders. The columns of the portico were reinforced, and both capitals and bases were enlarged to correspond to the increased diameter of the columns. Terra-cotta capitals were substituted for the old capitals of the columns and pilasters. The architrave and the frieze were

[..6 May 14, 1870.]   FRANK LESLIE'S ILLUSTRATED NEWSPAPER.   [May .

VIRGINIA—THE RICHMOND CALAMITY—CITIZENS AND FIREMEN REMOVING THE WOUNDED, THE DYING AND THE DEAD, FROM THE RUINS.—SKETCH TAKEN FROM THE WEST SIDE OF THE HALL OF DELEGATES, BY WM. L. SHEPPARD, OF RICHMOND.—SEE PAGE 134.

fig. 50 The Richmond Calamity—Citizens and Firemen Removing the Wounded, the Dying and the Dead, from the Ruins, by William Ludwell Sheppard, from *Frank Leslie's Illustrated Newspaper*, 14 May 1870. Virginia erected a building for the General Court in 1846, but after it burned in April 1865 the committee rooms above the House of Delegates chamber were converted to the courtroom that collapsed in the Capitol disaster of 1870.

rebuilt of stone and the cornice of terra-cotta. A marble floor was placed in the portico and marble treads on the new stairs, and the belt courses at the basement sill line and the first-floor line were made of stone instead of stucco. Inside, the niches of the rotunda were executed in marble instead of wood, and marble bases and wainscoting were introduced in the halls and rotunda. Noland and Baskervill stated also that the columns were given entasis when their diameter was increased, that the pediment was lowered somewhat, and that the modillions were increased in size. These statements are confirmed by a comparison with earlier drawings and photographs.

fig. 51 Expansion of the State Capitol, looking north. The extensive 1904–1906 repair and enlargement of the Capitol included a complete rebuilding of its roof, reinforcement of its columns, replacement of their capitals and bases, and construction of the south stairs.

fig. 52 Virginia State Capitol, 1922

Mr. Jefferson's Monument

We are now in a position to review the various changes that had taken place between the erection of the building and the addition of the wings, to determine how far the structure, as first erected, conformed to Jefferson's original design. That the completed Capitol conformed in general is as certain as that it differed in many particulars. The use of the Ionic order, the number of bays on front and side, the main proportions, the principal divisions of the interior, and many other details agreed with the model and with Jefferson's intentions. Accordingly, rather than specifying further agreements minutely, it will be simpler to note the points of difference, which include beside greater size and certain variations in proportion, the changes in the exterior approaches and steps, the addition of pilasters to the exterior walls, and the change in character of the door and window enframements.

It is no surprise that some differences should have crept in through adaptation to foundations previously laid, through modifications of the program, carelessness or defects of workmanship, local practices in building, and lack of understanding of the ideas of Jefferson and Clérisseau. Some of the stylistic changes, however, can be assigned to none of these causes. These are the expression of a different personality, which, like Jefferson and Clérisseau, was in some respects ahead of the time. This, as we shall see, can be no other than the Samuel Dobie, who has been mentioned by Edmund Randolph in 1786 as "our superintendant, and an adept in draughtmanship." In later times indeed he passed as the architect of the building, for there is no question that it is he who is meant when Mordecai speaks in his recollections of one "John Dobie . . . the architect of the Capitol."[1]

In a letter of William Hay to Governor Beverley Randolph, 11 May 1790, Dobie is referred to as "surveyor of the public Buildings," a title afterwards given by Jefferson to the architect of the Capitol in Washington.[2] Although Dobie was not employed by the Directors after 1794,[3] he was apparently still in Richmond in 1798 when Hay recommended him to inspect certain work under construction, "as the best Judge I know of work of this kind, & I must candidly confess that I do not consider myself as a competent Judge."[4] Concerning his origins and training nothing was said, and the author's inquiries of members of the Dobie family still in Virginia did not bring the desired information. We know, however, that he was already in the country as early as 1782,[5] and there seems no doubt that he came of a family that had long been in Virginia. A patent of land was issued to John Doby [Dobie] in 1683; the name of Dobie appears on marriage bonds of 1750 and 1761.[6]

In the original competition for the United States Capitol in 1791 Dobie submitted a design that throws light on his architectural knowledge and powers. It exhibits a square general mass with four porticoes and a dome over a central rotunda. The suggestion is obviously from Palladio's Villa Rotonda, but the scale is much greater and the details are modified in an interesting way. Two of the porticoes are octastyle and the rotunda is large enough to have an interior colonnade. The exterior dome, however, instead of having the semicircular form shown in Palladio's plate of the villa, is of true Roman shape, which implies a familiarity with classical forms very unusual at that time in America. Dobie was evidently a man of some independent knowledge and training, whose influence on the building of the Virginia Capitol must be reckoned with.

Among the individual differences between the design of the Capitol of Virginia and the execution, the greater size is readily explained by the necessity of conforming to the foundations already laid before Jefferson's design arrived. As one would expect from Edmund Randolph's letter, the length of the building corresponds to the length of the foundations and the width is less than that of those foundations but proportional to the width of the model. The general increase thus necessitated was approximately 10 percent, and the dimensions of the plan conform to this percentage with a very small margin of error. The heights, however, both of the columns and of the entablature are increased in greater ratio of about 14 percent. This makes the columns about nine and a half diameters high instead of nine, and thus the change can scarcely have been made in an attempt to improve the proportions. It resulted more probably from increases in the interior heights, which lengthened the pilasters and forced a proportional increase in the entablature. The pediment was raised again to the Palladian ratio that Jefferson had originally used, 2:9, one which occurs again in Dobie's design for the United States Capitol.

In the interior, Lybrock's 1858 drawings show rooms that differed in many respects from Jefferson's intentions: most notably, the Senate occupied the south end room of the main floor rather than a room on the second floor. Widening of the end rooms at the expense of the central rotunda made window placement within these rooms unbalanced, while the narrowing of the rotunda crowded out its intended colonnade and forced the use of brackets to support its gallery. Only the chamber of the House of Delegates on the north side of the principal floor was significantly enhanced: The Speaker's chair was placed in the middle of the north wall, and galleries were constructed at both ends of the room. The basilican colonnade was omitted in the courtroom above the House chamber, and the length of the Senate chamber, next to the portico on the main floor, was cut to create space for clerks' offices at the end of the room. Partition walls of the upper floor probably had been modified in the antebellum decades, as when the General Court moved to its own building in the 1840s, and initially the space occupied by the library certainly was not as extensive as suggested in Lybrock's drawings.

Another group of changes also are readily explained. These include the omission of the monumental flight of steps before the portico and the substitution of single flights at right angles to the building for the pairs shown on the model. Their object was undoubtedly to get more light and more offices in the basement. It is apparently to the side steps that an item in Samuel Dobie's account with the State refers: "For drawing plans . . . and directing the workmen in the years 1793 and 1794 in building the stone steps and stairs and finishing the Conference."[7] Before 1793 the plans had been sent away to L'Enfant in Washington and it is not surprising that the new plan of the steps should not have conformed to them. By 1793, also, the building had already been long enough in use to demonstrate that the side entrances were heavily used and that the small steps in front had only an aesthetic function, which had to give way before practical needs. Baskervill remembered quite distinctly that when the exterior plaster was removed from the sides in 1905, marks were found of stairs running as in the model. As Dobie wrote of building the stone steps, there may well have been previous temporary ones of wood having the form originally intended.

Another change traceable to Dobie is the addition of a parapet above the cornice—a feature not long preserved but attested by papers of the Directors. As we have seen, Dabney Minor was directed in May 1792 to whitewash the pedestals on the top of the Capitol, and in June of the same year occurs an item "3 Tonns of Lead for covering the Pedestal Cornice & Workmanship."[8] These statements can refer only to a parapet of pedestal form such as Dobie showed later on his design for the Capitol at Washington. The use of Vincenzo Scamozzi's Ionic capital on the exterior order may likewise be assigned to Dobie on similar grounds. They appear not only on his design for the Capitol of the United States but also in the interior finish of the building at Richmond, which was not shown in the drawings sent from abroad.

The most striking modification—which clearly evidences an intervention by someone exercising greater control over the design than was left to the ordinary craftsman of the day—was the addition of the pilasters at each bay along the sides and rear of the building. This was a step in the direction of a closer following of the classic prototype as well as of Palladian architecture in the grand manner, both of which we can attribute to Dobie. The pilasters belong certainly to the original construction; they are mentioned in the vouchers in 1792, were seen by La Rochefoucaud-Liancourt and Latrobe, and were found by Noland and Baskervill bonded into the walls. It is interesting to note that Dobie's design for the Capitol at Washington has a pilaster treatment exactly similar. The likelihood might be urged that Dobie derived this idea from the Virginia Capitol but, as there is not a vestige of evidence that the pilasters were ever included in the original design and as there is ample proof that Dobie had an independent knowledge of classical forms and a preference for them, it must be concluded that the pilasters were due to him in both cases.

One other stylistic change attracts attention: the substitution of enframements having an indefinably Greek flavor for the Louis XVI doors and windows of the plaster model. These formed part of the work of finishing the exterior in 1797–1798 at the time the stucco was laid on. At that date Dobie was no longer in the employ of the Virginia Directors, and his detail for the Washington Capitol design has nothing of this Greek touch. In Richmond and employed by the Directors at that very moment was the first representative of the Greek Revival to come to America, Benjamin Henry Latrobe. He was well versed in Greek forms, as his 1807 design for the *corps de garde* of the United States Capitol makes clear.[9] His first important commission in this country was the design of the Virginia State Penitentiary at Richmond, on which he was employed during

1797 and 1798. With the original drawings of the Capitol lacking, nothing could have been more natural than that state authorities should have applied to the best-qualified person at hand for a design for these missing details. Benjamin Henry Latrobe probably was responsible for framing the Capitol's door and windows in a style that anticipated the Greek Revival.

To complete our study of the executed building it remains only to examine those points not covered by the original drawings and the model, which, in the absence of sections, the builders were forced to decide for themselves. Most important of these was the method of covering the central hall. A dome was adopted, accommodated to the square room by flat, triangular soffits, naively unstructural but not unsatisfactory. The surface of the dome itself was decorated with segmental gores, such as those Dobie used in his proposed design for the Capitol of the United States. The interior detail for the most part presents nothing unexpected in late colonial woodwork. The Doric and Ionic orders of the House and Senate chambers were of stereotyped forms, with no trace of Adamesque influence and few of the ordinary native adaptations to the material. Only in the consoles of the doorways in the central hall was there evidence of the more direct classical influence sometimes appearing elsewhere in Dobie's work.

A curious evidence, to which there is now no danger of attaching too much significance, is offered by the railing about the rotunda opening. When the paint was removed from this at the time of the remodeling in 1904–1906, there was found, according to Baskervill, the name "Thomas Jefferson," very neatly carved, as if by a workman. In the absence of any other obvious motive for this, one may assume that it was a testimony to the common knowledge of Jefferson's part in the design.

The materials used in the building did not conform entirely to Jefferson's informal suggestions in his letter of 13 August 1785, but that was hardly to be expected. He had proposed that the columns and external architraves be of stone, the external cornice of wood, and the interior cornices and trim of plaster.[10] As constructed, the columns of the portico were of brick and according to Noland and Baskervill hollow like a well-curb. The main entablature was all of wood, the enframements of the openings were modeled in stucco, and the interior orders were of wood.

Considering the executed building as a whole, it is evident that much had been lost from Jefferson's original design with very little compensating gain. The proportions of the columns were greatly injured by the increase in their relative height, the relation between the rooms and the fenestration suffered, and the majestic columnar subdivision of the interior was abandoned without securing the delicate charm of typically colonial woodwork. The scale, to be sure, was further increased. While the pilasters tended to restore the unity of the walls and portico, and while the Greek doors and windows were more in advance of stylistic fashion, nevertheless some of the elegance and consistency of the original design were lost. In their predestined attempt to reach the classic ideal set them, Dobie and his comrades failed to strike fairly either their own goal or the less-ambitious mark of the humbler craftsmen. So far as the building succeeded, it was due to the underlying qualities with which Jefferson had endowed it at the first—qualities that make the building itself as truly his as the finished design sent from France. The use of the simple and crystalline temple form, the colossal order, the monumental disposition of the interior—the chief remains of Thomas Jefferson's ideas—are what give the Capitol of Virginia its novel dignity, its expressiveness of the democratic majesty of the new and sovereign republican state.

Revealing Jefferson's Model for the Capitol of Virginia

Thomas Jefferson's 1785–1786 plaster model stands as the purest embodiment of his vision for the Capitol of Virginia. It has been on view to Virginians for most of its existence, much of that time in the Capitol. It is difficult to imagine that an object so prominent, meaningful, and familiar could hold astonishing secrets for more than 200 years. Yet when a study was eventually made of the model, it recovered striking information, much of it lost for more than two centuries. In 1994, the Library of Virginia, the agency responsible for the model's care, commissioned the first thorough investigation, eventually followed by intensive conservation of the model in partnership with Colonial Williamsburg. The project became a mission to reveal the discoveries, at the same time preserving the complex physical layers of history manifest in the original (figs. 53–54).[1]

Jefferson, following the common practice of Parisian architects at the time, augmented Charles-Louis Clérisseau's drawings with "models of the front and side" in "plaister of Paris." He justified the additional expense by proclaiming the model "absolutely necessary for the guide of workmen not very expert in their art."[2] Jefferson chose as his model maker Jean-Pierre Fouquet (1752–1829), "an artist who had been employed many years in Greece . . . making models of the most celebrated remains of antient architecture in that country."[3] Fouquet proved himself a master *modeleur,* typically using a relatively small scale of 1:36 to construct plaster of Paris models characterized by perfectly scaled proportions and sharply defined detail.[4] Jefferson's model is the earliest-known extant example by Fouquet and is somewhat atypical of his work. Most of the approximately 100 documented models from the studios of Fouquet and his son François were miniature reconstructions of ancient temples made for the collections of wealthy antiquarians. Only eight were prototype models for new architectural designs and, of these, only Jefferson's design and one other became full-scale structures.[5]

In January 1786, Clérisseau finished his drawings and Jefferson sent them to Virginia. Fouquet probably worked from a second set of drawings, completing the model and packing it for shipping in June. Much to Jefferson's dismay, however, the model was not shipped until December, causing it to arrive in Virginia well after work had begun on the building. Nonetheless, both the drawings and the model apparently proved useful for the construction of the Capitol.

After the completion of the building, Fouquet's model stayed in Richmond, the only direct result of Jefferson's partnership with Clérisseau, as the architect's drawings were lost before the end of the eighteenth century. The model and base are approximately sixteen inches high, thirty-two inches long, and nineteen inches wide. Fouquet built the model at a smaller-than-usual scale of 1:60, or one inch to every five feet. He reinforced the plaster portico, side, and roof with internal iron rods, and he made the base of oak. In his instructions for unpacking the model, Fouquet mentioned "un cage de verre," a glass cover, now lost, that protected the delicate plaster surface of the model.[6]

fig. 53 Fouquet model before treatment, ca. 1994

fig. 54 Fouquet model after treatment, 2001

The fragile model experienced a history of change and repair. Most significant, a rear wall was added early in the model's Virginia history, in part, perhaps, to stabilize the structure. In 1829 and again in 1834, Philip Sturtevant, an accomplished stucco worker and carver, restored or repaired the model. His work probably included repairs to the roof, which had collapsed at some point. A crudely installed reinforcing bar and hastily applied plaster on the interior suggest that someone other than a skilled artisan made later undocumented repairs.[7] Jagged losses to the portico cornice appeared by the early twentieth century and were patched in 1975. Additional minor repairs were carried out in 1992.

Displayed in the Executive Mansion throughout much of the nineteenth century, the model received regular additions of paint. It apparently was placed in storage early in the twentieth century (probably because of construction projects at the Capitol and the Executive Mansion) and later stood in the entry hall of the Capitol rotunda, where it was displayed for most of the twentieth century as a white building with a gray roof.

In 1994, the Library of Virginia sent the model to Colonial Williamsburg's Department of Conservation for a painstaking evaluation. Structural stability of the repaired roof was the primary concern, but there were also questions raised by the overall appearance of the model. The paint exhibited pronounced *cracquelure* (crackling), the white surface was dingy, and the architectural detail was indistinct. The study sought to determine if overpainting obscured original detail, or if Fouquet had intended only to render an impression of the Jefferson-Clérisseau design.

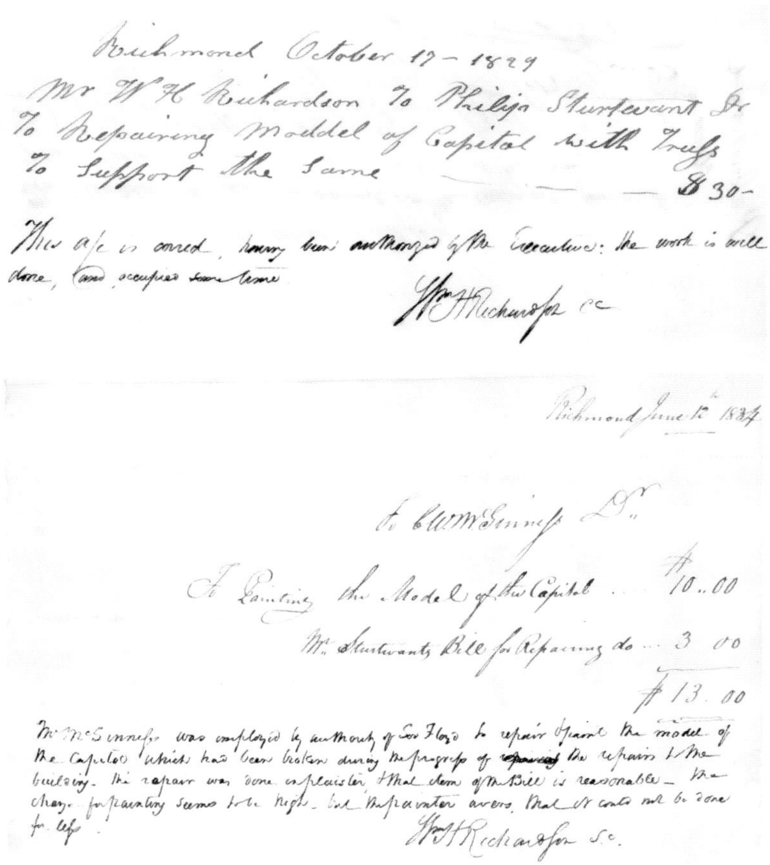
Richmond October 17 – 1829
Mr W H Richardson To Philip Sturtevant Dr
To Repairing Moddel of Capitol with Truss
To Support the Same — $30–
This a/c is correct, having been authorized by the Executive: the work is well done, and occupied some time
Wm H Richardson cc

Richmond June 1st 1834
To C W McGinnis Dr
To Painting the Model of the Capitol 10..00
Mr Sturtevants Bill for Repairing do 3 00
$13.00
Mr McGinnis was employed by authority of Gov Floyd to repair & paint the model of the Capitol which had been broken during the progress of the repairs to the building. the repair was done in plaister & the item of Mr Bill is reasonable — the charge for painting seems to be high — but the painter avers that it could not be done for less.
Wm H Richardson S.C.

fig. 55 Accounts of repairing and painting the model, 1829 and 1834

To evaluate the structure, Colonial Williamsburg had the Non-Destructive Evaluation Sciences Lab, at the NASA Langley Research Center, in Hampton, take X-ray images of the model. The images confirmed that the roof was stable, but this welcome news was overshadowed by a wonderful, unexpected byproduct of the examination—the appearance of astonishing architectural detail. Radiographs revealed precisely rendered classical door and window architraves including miniscule guttae (triangular pendants) beneath each window bracket; tiny fruits and foliage in the garlands ornamenting the tablets between the first- and second-story windows; and precise, miniature egg-and-dart moldings and other running patterns incorporated into the elaborate cornices (fig. 56). Ironically, these and other refined but faint images were visible only because of the layers of dense lead paint encasing the plaster ornament. When applied, the paint collected thickly in the recesses of the ornament and flowed away from projections. During

radiography the lead pigment absorbed more or less X-ray energy according to its variable thickness, resulting in X-ray images that revealed beautifully contrasting surface details.

A subsequent microscopic study of tiny paint samples from the surface of the model indicated that it bore anywhere from twelve to fifteen layers of paint above the plaster, each layer telling an interesting tale. Various colors appeared—a surprise to modern Virginians who know only a white Capitol. On the model only the uppermost layers (all probably dating from the twentieth century) appear white.

fig. 56 A reverse X ray reveals original details of the cornice.

Earlier paint layers, depending on their location on the model, are gray, buff, brown, yellow, black, and dark blue-green. This indicates that over the years, the model bore schemes of two or more colors at a time.

A study of Capitol images, ranging from an 1801 engraving to 1890s photographs, showed several multicolored paint schemes over the 200-plus years of the building's history. The earliest, detailed color image, a circa 1830 painting by William Goodacre, which is false in many respects, nonetheless reveals a color scheme strikingly similar to one of the earliest paint schemes on the model—yellow ocher walls with white columns, cornices, architraves, and other details. Later layers correspond to schemes on the Capitol building throughout the rest of the nineteenth century. In the 1890s, for instance, the Capitol walls were light gray while the window and door trim were much darker—a direct parallel to a scheme on the model evidently from the same period, found directly below the thick, white, twentieth-century paint. Apparently, each time the Capitol received a new color scheme, the model was painted to match. Consequently, the model undoubtedly bears a more comprehensive paint history of the Capitol than the heavily altered building itself.

A complex question arose over whether to remove the overpaint to reveal the model's remarkable original workmanship. After all, the original plaster was the surface Jefferson knew, the purest surviving evidence of his and Clérisseau's design. A committee of architectural scholars, Library of Virginia staff members, and the clerks of the House and Senate met to review the findings and discuss conservation options. The group affirmed the historic significance of the overpaint and acknowledged conservation concerns that its removal would risk additional physical damage to the delicate original plaster. Ultimately, they approved a plan to clean and conserve the original components of the model, leaving the historic paint intact as a document of Virginia architectural history. At the same time they approved a proposal for selective overpaint removal on the added rear wall to reveal several of the historic paint schemes. To interpret the discoveries made during radiography, they approved a plan to fabricate a detailed reproduction for exhibition alongside the original model.[8]

The project became two-faceted: a conservative treatment of the original model complemented by the fabrication of an accurate copy. The model would retain all generations of historic paint on its facade, side elevation, and roof. The Colonial Williamsburg conservators would clean the painted surfaces, remove and refill old patches, and apply new fills and inpaint to minimize the visibility of previous roof repairs. On the rear wall, conservation would reveal a chronology of five historic paint schemes, each in a vertical strip corresponding to one of the five window bays. Meanwhile, fabrication of the reproduction would take advantage of new technologies and historic modelmaking techniques to produce an accurate copy of the model as Jefferson knew it.

Prior to treatment and replication, additional research involved examination and photography of Fouquet models at the Victoria and Albert Museum (fig. 57) and the Sir John Soane's Museum in London,

fig. 57 Model of Tomb at Palmyra, attributed to Jean-Pierre Fouquet

and the Musée Carnavalet in Paris. This was followed by a comparative analysis of microsamples taken from several of the models. The findings provided insight into Fouquet's typical materials and methods and answered questions arising from the study of the few eighteenth-century references to architectural modelmaking. This helped sort out questions about the original appearance of Jefferson's model, distinguishing Fouquet's work from alterations and additions that occurred after the model arrived in Virginia.

The study of other Fouquet models also provided a clear vision for the fabrication of the reproduction. Except for their roofs, pavement, and a few other details, these structures bore no paint, and their delicately textured plaster surfaces varied from smooth to finely striated to grainy. Fouquet obviously had no intention of obscuring the fine details of his models. Other than its gray-painted roof, Jefferson's model likely arrived in Virginia with a pristine, white plaster surface. This is corroborated by Fouquet's inclusion of a cover for the model. Unlike paint, porous plaster surfaces become grimy unless covered, and the models that survive in their original vitrines (particularly those at London's Soane's Museum) maintain a clean, white appearance.[9]

Studying the plaster surfaces of the other Fouquet models also provided useful insight into the maker's techniques. The scant written references of the period indicate the use of molds, hand techniques, templates on soft material, and hand finishing of dry plaster with gouges and files. The surfaces of the Fouquets reflect this variety of techniques. Visible joints are rare, but several models exhibit slight joint lines between the bases of capitals and their columns, indicating they were fabricated separately, perhaps using different techniques. The regularity of the columns on each temple suggests they were made from molds taken from a single master column. The master was probably built up from soft plaster turned on a shaft against a template, as fine striations perpendicular to the axes of the columns may be residual evidence of the master's template. Meanwhile, elaborate Ionic, Corinthian, and Composite capitals were assembled from numerous tiny, molded components. Regular striations also appear on some of the wall surfaces, perhaps an indication of the hand tools used to achieve the final finish on the models.

fig. 58 Amy Fernandez uncovers a paint layer, 2001.

The inventory of Fouquet's studio, taken after his death in 1829, is frustrating for the lack of insight it offers into his techniques and tools. Most items mentioned are the products of his work, including models of buildings and columns, and six boxes of "various fragments of plaster architectural ornaments." Tool descriptions are minimal and vague, confirming only that Fouquet owned toolboxes, a vise, a saw, a plane, and fifteen molds to produce columns. Only the last item is instructive, because it indicates Fouquet's use of master molds to standardize his production of plaster columns.[10]

X-ray images showed that the rear wall of the Capitol model was not plaster at all, a feature distinguishing it from the other Fouquet models. Not only were the rear wall's windows, garlands, and cornices less refined than elsewhere, but the area bore the characteristic grain pattern of wood, unlike the consistent plaster core of the side wall, portico, and roof. An initial supposition held that Fouquet made the rear wall simpler than the rest of the model for economic reasons. After all, it bore all or nearly all the paint layers found elsewhere, so it was reasonable to assume it was part of the original structure. Jefferson, however, had written that the model would consist only of a side elevation and a portico. It was possible that the rear wall was a later addition. A one-eighth-inch-square sample of low-density, close-grained, gray-green wood from the inner surface of the wall held the answer. The greenish appearance was the telltale sign: it was tulip poplar, a common forest tree in Virginia that is not native to Europe. Microscopic examination confirmed the identification and supported the surprising conclusion: the rear wall was made in Virginia.

This revelation had two important ramifications. First, it upheld Jefferson's description of the model, thus informing the design of the reproduction. Second, it confirmed the Virginia origin of all but one of the paint layers on the walls, columns, and portico (the exception was an early, thin white

fig. 59 Overpaint removal on the model's rear wall reveals historic color schemes.

"touch-up" layer probably applied to disguise dirt). Because of the extensive history of paint on the rear wall, it also became apparent that the wall was added soon after the model had served its purpose in the building of the Capitol—perhaps when it took on new meaning as a historic object. Presumably, the wall both stabilized the roof and made the model more complete, thus more suitable to exhibit.

Additional paint analysis refined understanding of the historic paint schemes and revealed some striking new discoveries. For instance, two layers of dark blue-green painted paper were sandwiched in between the paint layers covering the window openings. One was characteristic of paper made before 1830 while the other dated between 1830 and 1870, dates useful in establishing the paint chronology. The paper also appears on the rectangular recesses above the second-floor windows. Its presence there confirmed that Virginians considered the recesses to represent attic windows well into the nineteenth century, even though the Capitol was built without a third floor. Careful experimental excavations of paint also revealed new information. On at least two of the paint schemes, including one of the earliest, traces of dark vertical and horizontal lines appeared on the walls. Examined with infrared light, a distinctive pattern of simulated ashlar emerged: the painter had applied fine lines of charcoal in careful imitation of stone blocks.[11]

After thoroughly evaluating the model's paint schemes, the Library of Virginia and Colonial Williamsburg selected five major schemes to reveal on the rear wall. Of the seven nineteenth-century schemes present, three dating from midcentury were similar, making the selection process easier. The final choices: a warm tan with white trim that probably dates from about 1800, the rich yellow ocher with

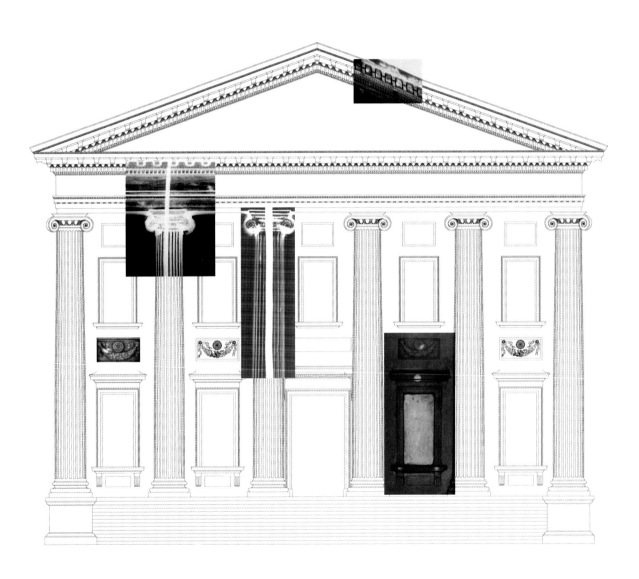

fig. 60 Composite illustration of a drawing by John Watson overlaid with X-ray images of a garland, column capital and entablature, column, cornice, and window and pilaster base

off-white trim likely dating from the 1820s, a medium tan dating from before the Civil War, a light buff or sand color probably from the 1870s, and a cool gray with dark trim that apparently dates from about 1890 (fig. 59). The conservation of the model greatly improved its appearance, preserving and interpreting the history of the artifact. Looking at the portico and side elevation, viewers see a cleaner, more intact structure, but the surface appears much as it has throughout the twentieth century (fig. 54). The rear wall, on the other hand, provides a chronology of the historic appearance of the Capitol model—and the Capitol itself—throughout the nineteenth century.

Interpreting the original appearance of the model was an equally important consideration in the project. By making an accurate set of drawings as well as a plaster reproduction, the conservators sought to retrieve the essence of Thomas Jefferson's design (fig. 60). The process was a painstaking amalgam of current imaging technologies, research into eighteenth-century classical architecture, and

fig. 61 Assembling the 2002 reproduction of the model

modern and historic modelmaking techniques. Numerous X-ray images of original model details, taken using special techniques to provide the most accurate dimensional information possible, served as the primary source of information. Where details were obscured or unclear in the X-ray images, conservators made informed interpretations guided by classical architectural drawing books. Two-dimensional computer drawings were prepared that will serve, along with the X-ray images, as the most accurate references to the original model. Meanwhile, three-dimensional patterns were made using both 3-D computer modeling/milling technology and traditional techniques of handcraftsmanship. The final casting process drew on the few scant references to historic plaster modelmaking techniques, evidence visible on the surfaces of Fouquet's other models, and clues discerned in X-ray images of the structure of the Capitol model.

Throughout the drawing and reproduction process, the project team was reminded constantly of Jean-Pierre Fouquet's skill and remarkable attention to detail. Modern technology and materials aided the fabrication of the reproduction, but Fouquet's precise workmanship continually challenged the process. Ultimately, the work of replicating the Virginia Capitol model left the project team with a profound sense of respect for Fouquet, who, using the limited techniques and materials available to him in the eighteenth century, so ably embodied in miniature Jefferson's architectural vision.[12]

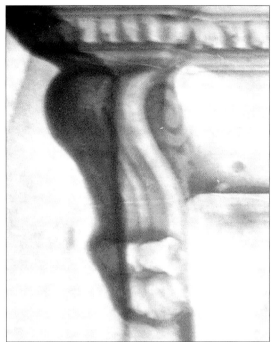

fig. 62 Reverse X rays delineate an iron reinforcing rod in the door cornice and the spirals and leaf forms of the console.

And what exactly was Jefferson's architectural vision for the Virginia Capitol? How much of that vision was influenced by Clérisseau? How much did they draw on the Maison Carrée for the design, and what other architectural sources did they use? These are a few of the perennial questions surrounding the Capitol design, and one might assume they could be readily addressed with our new awareness of the precise academic detail of the "primary document"—the Fouquet model. From Jefferson's own words as well as the research of Fiske Kimball and others, it has long been apparent that the Maison Carrée was but one of the inspirations for the Capitol design. The newly revealed Capitol model will help confirm some of the others, as the X-radiographs permit new, more accurate measurements of the elements comprising it—useful in determining their proportional relationships and, possibly, their origins. This new information provides scholars with tantalizing opportunities for exploring the intent of Jefferson and the contribution of Clérisseau.

To be sure, the nature and scale of the model present a few hindrances to the study. When magnified for interpretive purposes, Fouquet's miniature artisanry in plaster reveals certain departures from ideal academic form and proportion. Some deviations result from unavoidable vagaries in Fouquet's handcraftsmanship, however precise. Moldings vary slightly in dimension and profile at either end of cornices, and some of the tiniest moldings have indefinite profiles. Dentils also vary in width and spacing.

Other deviations may have been intentional. Architrave fillets, for instance, appear slightly wider than expected, possibly to make them more visible to the viewer at such a small scale. In addition,

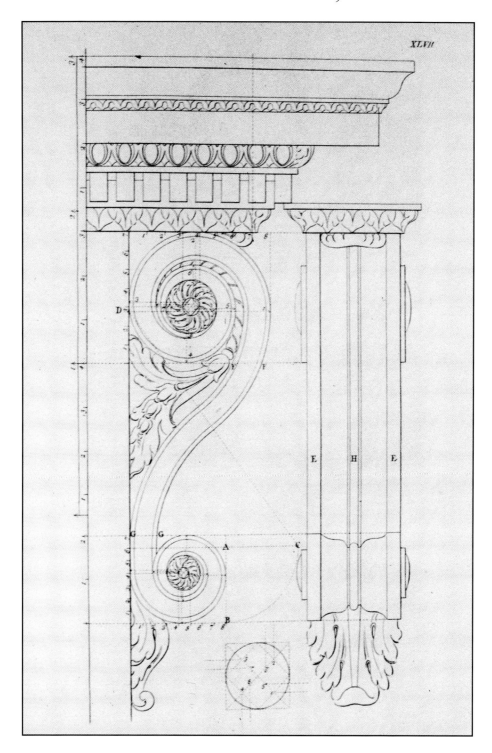

fig. 63 Plate 47 of Gibbs's *Rules for Drawing* illustrates many of the same console elements that Jefferson used in the Capitol design. The two designers' cornice profiles are virtually identical.

Fouquet necessarily simplified some of the ornamental features to accommodate the small scale of the model. His door consoles are little more than a half-inch high, so it was astounding to discover their well-delineated faces in the X-ray images, complete with double-ogee and bead molding and a well-formed baluster and acanthus leaf at the base of each scroll (fig. 62). It was even more remarkable to find evidence of spirals, leaves, and rosettes on their sides. Nonetheless, Fouquet's consoles are simple in comparison to possible source examples in James Gibbs's *Rules for Drawing the Several Parts of Architecture* and Palladio's *Four Books*, both owned by Jefferson, as well as Vincenzo Scamozzi's 1615 *L'Idea dell'Architettura Universale*, a work probably available to Clérisseau.[13] Scamozzi's is closest in proportion while Gibbs's is most similar in ornament—and Gibbs's "scroll" supports a cornice (fig. 63) with a profile nearly identical to that above the model's consoles. But the small scale and simplified forms of Fouquet's work preclude an unquestionable attribution.

The deviations and simplifications of classical prototypes found on the model, whether intentional or resulting from the limitations of Fouquet's craftsmanship, may complicate the process of identify-

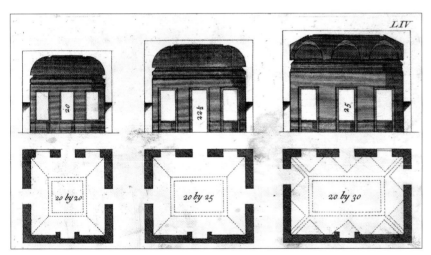

fig. 64 Coved ceilings from Gibbs's Plate 54. *fig. 65* Jefferson designed a similar coved ceiling for the Capitol, as seen in the model before restoration.

ing sources for the design. Nonetheless, as the following examples attest, careful observation may provide insight into the design sources—and possibly the design options—put forward by Jefferson.

First, X-ray images of the model reveal a curious discrepancy between the entablature on the portico facade and that on both sides of the portico and the side elevation. Although the modillions, dentils, and molding profiles are identical, only the facade moldings bear the rich egg-and-dart, bead-and-reel, and water-leaf ornamentation. It is unlikely that Fouquet fabricated plain moldings on the sides of the model simply as a cost-saving measure: complex patterns prepared for the facade entablature would have served for the sides at little extra expense. Did Jefferson intend for the Capitol to be built in this manner? Possibly, as his much later designs for the entablatures of Pavilions I and II at the University of Virginia show a distinct parallel: their facade friezes are richly ornamented while their sides are plain.[14] It is also plausible that the differences reflect Jefferson's architectural idealism tempered by fiscal pragmatism. He undoubtedly envisioned the Virginia Capitol with the rich ornamentation of the model's facade, but was fully aware of the financial constraints faced by the young commonwealth. He may have intended the plain entablature as a significantly less expensive option for the builders of the Capitol. Understandably, they chose the simpler design.

New measurements of the model—shorn of paint by X-radiography—also confirm Jefferson's Palladianism as a major influence in the Capitol design. For instance, one of the model's features normally

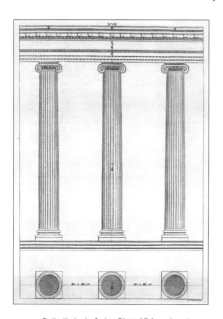

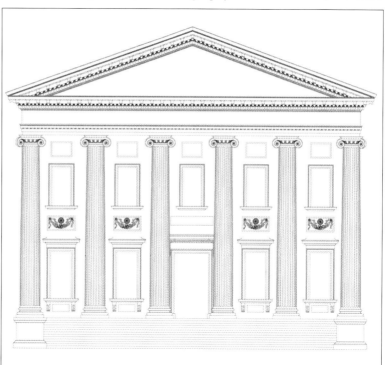

fig. 66 Palladio Ionic Order, Plate 17 from Leoni. *fig. 67* John Watson's drawing of the portico emphasizes the model's column proportion and intercolumniation.

hidden from viewers—its airy coved portico ceiling—exemplifies the model's conformation to Palladian rules of proportion (fig. 65). The ceiling form departs from the celebrated prototype for the Capitol design, the Maison Carrée, which has a portico ceiling divided into numerous ornamented square coffers.[15] Instead, the architects chose to proportion the interior portico space as if it were an arched chamber, following a simple rule put forth by Palladio for determining the height of a coved ceiling: "a height proportional to the length and breadth together may be easily found, by joining both the two Lines of the length and breadth into one Line, which being divided by the middle, the one half will give exactly the height of the *Arch*."[16]

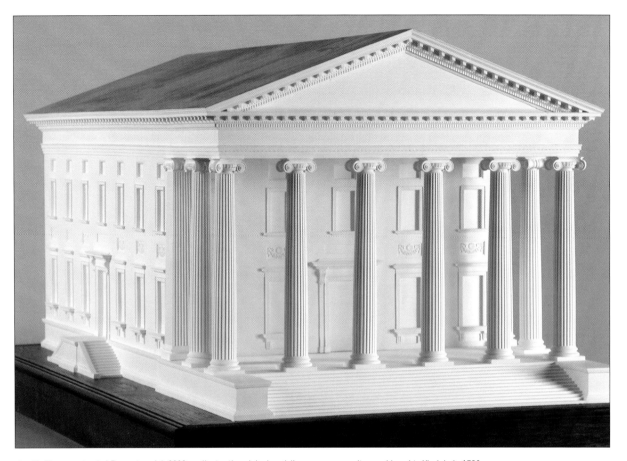

fig. 68 The reconstructed Fouquet model, 2002, replicates the original model's appearance as it was shipped to Virginia in 1786.

Considering the inevitable inaccuracies resulting from handcraftsmanship, it is remarkable that the actual measured height of Fouquet's portico ceiling is within 2 percent of the height calculated using Palladio's rule.

Even more telling, a study of the model's portico confirms that the arrangement and proportions of its columns (figs. 66–67) follow Palladian specifications Jefferson proposed in his "Notes explicatives des plans du Capitole pour l'état de la Virginie," a document he prepared before meeting Clérisseau. Jefferson apparently drew on the Ionic order presented in Chapter 16, Book 1, of Giacomo Leoni's version of *The Architecture of A. Palladio*. Palladio, following the system proposed by Vitruvius, based his proportional relationships on a unit known as the module—a measurement of the diameter of the lower portion of each column. Palladio proclaimed the ideal Ionic column to be nine modules high. Jefferson proposed the same relationship for the portico columns mentioned in his "Notes," and the Capitol model columns deviate only slightly from this 9:1 ratio: their height (197.9 mm) is 8.84 times their diameter. Likewise, the model's intercolumniation (the ratio of the space between columns to column diameter) is 2.22, nearly the $2\frac{1}{4}$ modules proclaimed by Palladio as the "most beautiful and commodious of all Inter-columns, which Vitruvius calls Eustyle."[17] Indeed, in his

"Notes," Jefferson appears to echo Palladio's text as well as his proportioning, proposing the Capitol intercolumniation to be "approximately the Eustyle of $2\frac{1}{4}$ diameters."[18] He carried forward the same arrangement in visual form in his final elevation of the proposed portico.

By contrast, the columns in Clérisseau's drawings of the Maison Carrée—with typically Corinthian proportions ten modules high and an intercolumniation of 1.74—appear unrelated to those of the Capitol model. Other ancient temples mentioned by Jefferson as inspirations for the Virginia Capitol design also show distinctly different proportions. This includes the Temple of Portunus (known as Fortuna Virilis in the eighteenth century), which was the apparent source for the model's column capitals and the architrave directly above them.[19] Indeed, it is now clear that Jefferson intended for the Virginia Capitol to display the proportions of the Ionic order he encountered in Leoni's version of Palladio, even after meeting Clérisseau and extolling the Maison Carrée as "the best morsel of antient architecture now remaining."[20] Perhaps more than anywhere else on the model, Jefferson's unabashed Palladianism is manifest in the proportioning and arrangement of its columns.

Some features of the Capitol model may never be fully explained, but the new findings gained from X-radiography, from paint and plaster analysis, and from investigations associated with the replication process have already refined our understanding of the Capitol design and opened new avenues for study. What now is known challenges a few of the assumptions Fiske Kimball made so many years ago in his groundbreaking research. Nothing, however, refutes Kimball's essential thesis

fig. 69 Temple of Portunus (known as Fortuna Virilis in the eighteenth century) was the apparent source for the model's column capitals and the architrave directly above them.

that Thomas Jefferson was the primary architect of Virginia's Capitol. As conserved, the original model will maintain its integrity as an artifact, serving not only as an embodiment of Jefferson's design but also as a document of historic changes to the Virginia Capitol throughout the nineteenth and twentieth centuries. Meanwhile, the new drawings and the reproduction in plaster will foster public understanding of Jefferson's role in the development of American Neoclassicism and reflect his vision for the noble purposes of architecture.

We now see Jefferson's conception for the Capitol with a much clearer eye, as we view for the first time in generations the vision of classical refinement and sophistication he brought to his Capitol design. From its overall plan to its finest details, the Capitol model once again attests to Jefferson's resolve to draw on classical antiquity to "furnish a model whereon to form the taste"[21] of the American public for the buildings of a new democracy.

"An Intelligent Regard to the Model"

In 1798 workmen covered the exterior brick walls of the Capitol with a long-awaited finishing coat of stucco, some ten years after the General Assembly had begun meeting there. Although this act may be considered the "completion" of the Capitol, throughout the nineteenth century the building's exterior witnessed changes in appearance and in architectural detail. Old photographs and renderings (including those reproduced in this volume) reveal variations in the size and type of windows placed within the pediment and basement, as well as the alteration of the stairways at the east and west entrances. Of particular interest is the repeated change in the color of the building's exterior walls and trim. Early in the 1800s the Capitol exterior was painted ochre; by the Civil War its walls were painted and scored to resemble stone; and by the end of the century the Capitol was a pale gray, its architectural details highlighted in dark brown. Little detailed information survives about the changes that interior spaces underwent in the nineteenth century. In the decades before the Civil War several interior modifications occurred, brought about by revised state constitutions in 1830 and in 1851 that enlarged the Senate and increased its meeting-space needs. The best and most-complete measured drawings of the Capitol's antebellum interior were not made until 1858, and only a handful of photographs document the interior during the period between the Civil War and the renovations of 1904–1906.

Had the Civil War not intervened, significant changes contemplated for the Capitol in the 1850s would probably have been implemented. In December 1849 and January 1850 the House of Delegates examined a plan to remove the side entrances and erect a proper stairway to the south portico at an estimated cost of $4,000. A few years later Samuel Freeman, superintendent of public buildings, formally recommended the construction of "a flight of granite steps [across] the entire length of the front of the portico. Under these steps apartments might be constructed as receptacles for wood and coal, now much needed, and also water closets." With broad new stairs to the portico, Freeman's proposal would have continued with "the removal of the steps on both sides of the building, the conversion of the principal doors into windows, and the change of the present [basement] entrances under these steps into handsome doors." Freeman believed these changes would "improve the appearance of the capitol, give it a more imposing and elevated look, and remove unsightly steps from its sides."[1]

Similar ideas appear in the extensive set of plans drawn in 1858 by Albert Lybrock for Governor Henry A. Wise. Lybrock, a Prussian living in Richmond, had designed the Morson's Row townhouses, facing the northeast corner of Capitol Square; the Ballard House hotel, several blocks east of Capitol Square; and James Monroe's Gothic Revival tomb at Hollywood Cemetery. He also supervised construction of the United States Post Office and Customs House just south of Capitol Square.[2] Lybrock's drawings show both existing conditions at the Capitol and proposals for revisions to the interior and exterior. Although his proposals were never implemented, Lybrock's measured drawings, preserved at the Library of Virginia, constitute an invaluable record of the Capitol as it stood at midcentury.[3]

As early as 1834 superintendents of public buildings had admitted their anxiety about the extreme length of inadequately supported floor joists and the resulting sagging of the Capitol's upper floors. In the 1850s further concerns were expressed about the possible decay and weakening of structural timbers. Postponement of major repairs, brought on in part by the Civil War and its aftermath, led to the "Capitol Disaster" of 27 April 1870. A crowd had gathered that day in the Supreme Court of Appeals, meeting in the room above the House of Delegates, to hear the decision on a contested Richmond mayoral race. The balcony in the courtroom collapsed onto the floor, which then collapsed into the House of Delegates chamber below. In the wake of this tragedy, in which at least 63 people died and more than 240 were injured, state officials examined the Capitol carefully, and then repaired and reconstructed the damaged rooms. City officials, fearful that a similar catastrophe might occur in the nearby City Hall designed by Robert Mills, demolished the building in 1874 and replaced it with the structure (completed in 1894) known today as Old City Hall.[4] A year after the Capitol disaster, Sherwin McRae published the first written history of the Capitol. Recognizing the architectural and historic significance of the original design, McRae urged that "in the repairing and adornment of the exterior of the Capitol, an intelligent regard should be had to the model. . . . Prudence, economy and taste . . . demand that whatever is done beyond mere preservation, shall contribute to conform the building to Mr. Jefferson's model."[5]

By 1900 the need for refurbishing and fireproofing the Capitol had become obvious to a generation of Virginians increasingly aware of the building's historic significance. On the eve of his retirement from office in 1902, Governor James Hoge Tyler, of Pulaski County, renewed his recommendations "made on several previous occasions in regard to the necessity of repairs to the Capitol. . . . To lose this historic building and the almost priceless statue of Washington which it contains would be an irreparable loss to the State."[6]

Tyler's successor, Andrew Jackson Montague, of Danville, repeated the plea in February 1902. The General Assembly agreed with Governor Montague's blunt statement that "the condition of the Capitol building is a reproach to the State" and appropriated $100,000 for interior and exterior repair and renovation. The assembly stipulated that "there be no alteration in the general design of this historic building any further than may be necessary."[7]

That spring Montague convened a five-member Capitol Building Commission that invited six architecture firms to submit proposed designs for repairing, fireproofing, and enlarging the Capitol. After rejecting four of the six submissions outright, the commission invited the remaining two firms—Frye and Chesterman of Lynchburg, and Noland and Baskervill of Richmond—to submit a composite plan that the commission adopted on 23 May 1902. This plan encountered opposition in both the Senate and the House of Delegates, but since the House liked the idea of new wings, the commission agreed to accept the wings concept as proposed by Norfolk architect John Kevan Peebles. After the assembly had received plans for the wings from the architects, however, agreement still could not be reached, so the proposals were withdrawn and the commission ceased to meet after November 1903.[8]

Governor Montague endorsed the proposal at the opening of the 1904 General Assembly session with a recommendation "that wings be added to the present building in accordance with plans which have been submitted." In March the General Assembly appropriated $250,000 for the project, and in August 1904 work began in the vacated Capitol. The exterior stairways and all the interior brickwork were torn out (except for the south half of the basement) and the bricks were salvaged for use in the rebuilt foundations and basement walls. Workers installed structural steel, fireproofing materials, and new ventilation flues throughout the gutted building. They built a fireplace and chimney in the governor's office, created a new basement entrance at the north end, rebuilt two interior staircases, and installed a new elevator. According to architectural historian Karen Lang Kummer, "only selected portions of the interior woodwork were salvaged, . . . reconditioned and reused: the trim around the openings of the first-floor rotunda; the door and arch trim, gallery balustrade and cornice of the second-floor rotunda; cornices at the ceiling and around the base of the dome; the face and balustrade of the gallery, the pilaster bases and capitals, and the cornice in the hall of the House of Delegates; and the pilasters and cornice in the Senate chamber." Replacement cornices and other details were fabricated in plaster. Except for windows in the basement that could be repaired, all the old windows and doors and their frames were replaced throughout the building.[9]

Outside, workers removed and replaced all the old stucco, built the long-anticipated south stairway with granite treads, repaved the portico floor in marble, and reinforced the columns, giving them entasis (a slight vertical curve to the column shaft) and enlarging their capitals and bases. John Kevan Peebles, chosen by the legislature to share project supervision with the Lynchburg and Richmond architecture firms, provided the muted Classical Revival design of the new wings that were linked to the original building with recessed hyphens. Visually echoing Jefferson's original design, Peebles intended to "disturb no lines of the present structure, which will be left as it is, a central mass to dominate the wings." Smaller in size and scale, subordinate to the main building, and covered with low roofs behind solid balustrades, the wings were carefully designed to accentuate the historic Capitol, not compete with it. Peebles noted,

> I am aware that there are some who will hold up their hands in horror and consider this desecration, . . . and I respectfully submit that if this addition in any way marred the present building and its surroundings, I would withdraw the suggestion. . . . I grant no man precedence in regard for the historic structures of Virginia. There are none who would stay the hand of the innovator more quickly than I, but in laying before you this suggestion, I feel

that it is the correct one, that it promises all you ask, and that Mr. Jefferson himself, if he were present, would approve it.[10]

The renovation begun in 1904 was completed in sixteen months at a total cost of $244,752.75. The General Assembly reoccupied the enlarged Capitol in January 1906, with the Senate meeting in the new west wing and the House of Delegates in the east. Agricultural exhibits from the Saint Louis World's Fair were placed in the Old Hall of the House of Delegates, and the reconfigured old Senate chamber was converted into a hearing room.[11]

In 1927 the General Assembly appropriated $5,000 to restore the Old Hall of the House of Delegates "to its former condition, as far as possible." Completed in 1929, the project re-created the chamber where Aaron Burr was tried in 1807, where Robert E. Lee accepted command of the Army of Northern Virginia in 1861, and where the Confederate House of Representatives met from 1861 until 1865. The chamber features life-size statues of Robert E. Lee and Henry Clay, joined by busts of Jefferson Davis, Patrick Henry, Sam Houston, Thomas Jonathan "Stonewall" Jackson, Joseph Eggleston Johnston, Fitzhugh Lee, Richard Henry Lee, Cyrus Hall McCormick, John Marshall, George Mason, Matthew Fontaine Maury, Alexander Hamilton Stephens, James Ewell Brown "J.E.B." Stuart, and George Wythe. The old Senate Chamber, refurbished in 1954, once housed the Confederate Senate. Louis Eugène Lami's monumental painting depicting the defeat of the British at Yorktown has hung in the chamber since 1878.[12]

The last major renovation of the Capitol was undertaken between 1962 and 1964 after several studies had been made of possible enlargements to the building. The chief structural change was the widening of the hyphens connecting the original building to the House and Senate wings. The hyphens' exterior staircases were replaced and enclosed on the south side and removed on the north side to enable construction of committee and conference rooms. Offices and committee rooms were also installed in the fourth-floor attic of the original building, necessitating the modification of old skylights. Other improvements included replacement of the metal roof; interior painting and refurbishment; the installation of a new elevator and the extension of the old elevator to the fourth floor; and the modernization of the building's electrical, plumbing, heating, and air-conditioning systems.[13]

Regular maintenance and repair of the Capitol have continued since the 1960s refurbishment. By the end of the twentieth century the Capitol was transformed into an electronic workplace. An automation project, completed in the autumn of 1999, outfitted the chambers for the House of Delegates and the Senate with upgraded sound systems and the technological infrastructure to support a network of computer interfaces and electronic-voting systems. Laptop computers were distributed to members of the legislature, and E-mail and Web sites have become major sources of communication. The next projects planned for the Capitol will upgrade support for electronic systems and overhaul the aging heating and cooling equipment. The clerk of the House and the clerk of the Senate have been instrumental in developing a consistently high level of care and conservation for the state's art collection housed in the Capitol. Professional conservators are regularly consulted for the repair and maintenance of such treasures as the life-size marble statue of George Washington by Jean-Antoine Houdon and the original 1786 model of the Capitol.

In 1999 the General Assembly created the Capitol Square Preservation Council, a fourteen-member body that includes the clerks of the House and Senate, the secretary of Administration, and individuals representing historical, architectural, landscape, gardening, and cultural organizations from throughout the state. The full Council meets quarterly, and an executive director conducts its ongoing work. The legislation set the Council's responsibilities: "With regard to the architectural, historical, archaeological and landscape features of Capitol Square and antiquities contained therein, the Council shall . . . develop plans and recommendations for their maintenance and preservation and for the enhancement of their historical and architectural integrity." The Council is also charged with assessing current conditions on Capitol Square, developing educational opportunities, and reviewing proposals that are "structural or architectural in nature."[14]

Visitors to Richmond more than two centuries after South Carolina native William Loughton Smith no longer encounter the sight he recorded in 1790—Virginia's "immense Capitol, towering above the Town on a lofty eminence, . . . which overlooks the whole Town, river, and adjoining country." For more than two hundred years the Capitol has stood as an architectural monument and as the active seat of Virginia's government. Richmond's landscape has changed considerably from the nineteenth century, when the Capitol was the dominant feature of the city's skyline. Yet once visitors make their way off the interstate highways and beyond the downtown skyscrapers, as they approach Capitol Square they still share with Smith and his contemporaries the experience of "a magnificent building."[15]

WRITTEN BY JON KUKLA AND
SARAH SHIELDS DRIGGS
VIRGINIA STATE LIBRARY AND ARCHIVES
1989

REVISED BY JAMES E. WOOTTON
CAPITOL SQUARE PRESERVATION COUNCIL
2002

Notes

INTRODUCTION TO THE 2002 EDITION

1. Quoted from Jefferson to Randolph, Papers of Thomas Jefferson, 1606–1902, Series 1, General Correspondence, 1651–1827, 1 Aug. 1785–1785–90, pp. 2533–2535 (images 361–363), microfilm and American Memory, Historical Collections for the National Digital Library online database, Library of Congress, Manuscript Division, Washington, D.C. (hereafter cited as LC). See also *The Papers of Thomas Jefferson*, ed. Julian P. Boyd et al. (Princeton, N.J.: Princeton University Press, 1950–), 8:538 (hereafter cited as Boyd, *Jefferson Papers*). The same sentiment regarding the Virginia State Capitol appears in Jefferson to James Madison, 20 Sept. 1785; see Boyd, *Jefferson Papers*, 8:535. The present reprint has come about because of the inspiring work on the Jefferson-Fouquet model of the Capitol conducted by F. Carey Howlett, former Director of Conservation, Colonial Williamsburg Foundation. I am indebted to Ray Bonis, Assistant Archivist, Special Collections and Archives, James Branch Cabell Library, Virginia Commonwealth University; Bryan Clark Green, Architectural Historian, Virginia Department of Historic Resources; and Mark R. Wenger, Architectural Research Department, Colonial Williamsburg Foundation, for generous assistance with sources; and to Monica Rumsey, my editor, for her perennial helpfulness. The following essay often draws on master's theses. No one knows better than the present writer that one must use even excellent theses with great caution. Those cited here range from the superb to the painfully flawed, but they are all essential for an understanding of Jefferson's Capitol.

2. Barbara C. Batson, Exhibitions Coordinator at the Library of Virginia, has restored the correct form of this passage ("is on the model of the temples") from "An Account of the Capitol in Virginia," in Papers of Thomas Jefferson, 1785 [*sic*], Series 1, General Correspondence, 1651–1827, 1 Aug. 1785–1785–90, pp. 2956–2957 (images 1007–1008), LC. The misquotation "is the model of the Temples" apparently entered the Jefferson literature with Henry A. Washington, who published a nine-volume compilation of Jefferson's writings in the 1850s (*The Writings of Thomas Jefferson*, ed. H. A. Washington [Washington, D.C.: Published by Taylor & Maury, 1853–1854], 9:446). Kimball, however, correctly transcribed "on the model" in his 1915 article, "Thomas Jefferson and the First Monument of the Classical Revival in America," *Journal of the American Institute of Architects* 3 (Sept. 1915): 376. The misquotation matters because it sounds like an eighteenth-century turn of phrase embodying some meaning lost on twenty-first-century readers.

3. I thank Lauren Weiss Bricker, Assistant Professor of Architecture, California State Polytechnic University, Pomona, for her assistance with the literature on Fiske Kimball. On Kimball, see Bricker, "Kimball, Fiske," *American National Biography*, ed. John A. Garraty and Mark C. Carnes (New York: Oxford University Press, 1999), 12:675–676; Bricker, "American Backgrounds: Fiske Kimball's Study of Architecture in the United States," in *The Early Years of Art History in the United States: Notes and Essays on Departments, Teaching, and Scholars*, ed. Craig Hugh Smyth and Peter M. Lukehart (Princeton, N.J.: Department of Art and Archaeology, Princeton University, 1993), 123–132; Bricker, "The Contributions of Fiske Kimball and Talbot Faulkner Hamlin to the Study of American Architectural History" (Ph. D. diss., University of California, Santa Barbara, 1992); Bricker, "The Writings of Fiske Kimball: A Synthesis of Architectural History and Practice," in *The Architectural Historian in America*, Studies in the History of Art, 35, Center for Advanced Study in the Visual Arts, Symposium Papers 19, ser. ed. Elisabeth Blair MacDougall (Washington, D.C.: National Gallery of Art, 1990), 215–235; Joseph Dye Lahendro, "Fiske Kimball: American Renaissance Historian" (Master of Architectural History thesis, University of Virginia, 1982); Mary Kane, *A Bibliography of the Works of Fiske Kimball*, ed. Frederick Doveton Nichols (Charlottesville: University of Virginia Press, 1959); and George Roberts and Mary Roberts, *Triumph on Fairmount: Fiske Kimball and the Philadelphia Museum of Art* (Philadelphia and New York: J. B. Lippincott, 1959). Kimball submitted his dissertation, "Thomas Jefferson and the First Monument of the Classical Revival in America" (University of Michigan, 1915) in printed form. With only minor changes, he used the same printing plates to publish his article "Thomas Jefferson and the First Monument of the Classical Revival in America," *Journal of the American Institute of Architects* 3 (Sept. 1915): 371–381; (Oct.): 421–433; (Nov.): 473–491. He almost immediately published a condensed statement of his conclusions in his book *Thomas Jefferson, Architect: Original Designs in the Collection of Thomas Jefferson Coolidge, Junior* (Boston: Printed for Private Distribution by the Riverside Press, Cambridge, 1916); reprinted under the title *Thomas Jefferson, Architect: Original Designs in the Coolidge Collection of the Massachusetts Historical Society*, with a new introduction by Frederick Doveton Nichols (New York: Da Capo Press, 1968); see esp. 40–43, 142–148 (nos. 110–117).

4. Quotations from Kimball, "Thomas Jefferson and the First Monument," are on 371 and 491.

5. Ibid. See esp. 379–381 (quotation on 381). The key document is Jefferson to James Buchanan and William Hay, 26 Jan. 1786, quoted by Kimball on 379–380, and now authoritatively published in Boyd, *Jefferson Papers*, 9:220–223. Jefferson scarcely had a reason or the time to detail the ins and outs of the evolution of

the design for his correspondents, and this fact probably accounts for some blurring of the story. In the Buchanan and Hay letter, however, Jefferson was unquestionably disingenuous. Faced with having to talk the Directors of the Public Buildings into reworking the Capitol foundations to accommodate his design, which he was sending very late, he took a strong stance: he wrote as if he had chosen the Maison Carrée at the outset as the ideal model for the Richmond statehouse. See Kimball, "Thomas Jefferson and the First Monument," 428, on Jefferson's maneuvering to ensure the faithful execution of his design.

6. Kimball published the Design 1 drawings in "Jefferson and the Public Buildings of Virginia: II. Richmond, 1779–1780," *Huntington Library Quarterly* 12 (May 1949): 303–310.

7. Kimball quoted the "Account of the Capitol" in "Thomas Jefferson and the First Monument" on 376. Unsurprisingly, Kimball's seminal work also included various slips, two of which must be noted here. Kimball misinterpreted as non-Jeffersonian the exterior "modern Ionic" capitals popularized by Vincenzo Scamozzi, and he indulged in a Jefferson's-memory-was-deceived argument to do this (432 n. 1, 483). And, misunderstanding the crudely proportioned Adamesque Tuscan tabernacle frames of the facades as Greek Revival, Kimball attributed these to Latrobe (484), who had no hand in the construction of the Capitol whatsoever.

8. The added illustration at the end of the epilogue on page 94 in the 1989 edition of *The Capitol of Virginia: A Landmark of American Architecture* (Richmond: Virginia State Library and Archives, 1989), 94, signaled the preparation of inestimably valuable measured drawings by the Historic American Buildings Survey in 1988. Virginia State Capitol, Richmond, Va., Historic American Buildings Survey, HABS, VA, 44-RICH, 9-, American Memory, Historical Collections for the National Digital Library online database, Prints and Photographs Division, LC.

9. Sarah Shields Driggs, one of the assistant editors of *The Capitol of Virginia* (1989) and a 1987 recipient of a master's degree in architectural history at the University of Virginia, flatly asserted to me in Nov. 1990 that Kimball's sequence for the drawings did not make sense. With perfect hindsight I can only applaud her acuity.

10. Sommer's paper, entitled "Thomas Jefferson and the Reform of Virginia Architecture," was presented at "Classicism: Visions and Revisions, 1740–1990," Third Annual Symposium, Department of Architectural History, University of Virginia, Charlottesville, 1990. Sommer's major published statement on Jefferson's architecture—one of the few learned discussions of the subject to appear during the 1970s—is "Thomas Jefferson's First Plan for a Virginia Building," in *Papers on American Art*, ed.

John C. Milley (Maple Shade, N.J.: Edinburgh Press for The Friends of Independence National Historical Park, 1976), 87–112. Compare "Thomas Jefferson and the First Monument," 428, and esp. 491, for Kimball's belief that Jefferson "broke" with Palladianism.

11. Kimball, "Thomas Jefferson and the First Monument," 430, esp. n. 1; Geneviève Cuisset, "Jean-Pierre et François Fouquet, Artistes Modeleurs," *Gazette des Beaux-Arts*, 6 period, vol. 115 (May–June 1990): 227–240. On Fouquet, see also James Yorke, "Tiny Temples of Mr. Nash," *Country Life* 195 (8 Feb. 2001): 66–67, and Werner Szambien, *Le Musée d'Architecture* (Paris: Picard, 1988), esp. 127–129. F. Carey Howlett kindly helped me with the literature on Fouquet.

12. Thomas J. McCormick, *Charles-Louis Clérisseau and the Genesis of Neo-Classicism* (New York: Architectural History Foundation; Cambridge, Mass., and London, Eng.: MIT Press, 1990). The coverage of the Virginia State Capitol appears in chap. 9, "Clérisseau, Thomas Jefferson, and the Virginia State Capitol, 1785–90," 191–199, which subsequent publications have rendered obsolete and which was flawed by obvious misstatements, such as the assertion (199) that the final treatment of the exterior windows and the change from the Corinthian Order of the Maison Carreé to the Ionic were Clérisseau's doing.

13. For my summary of Jefferson's architecture, see Brownell, Calder Loth, William M. S. Rasmussen, and Richard Guy Wilson, *The Making of Virginia Architecture* (Richmond: Virginia Museum of Fine Arts, 1992), chap. 2, "Laying the Groundwork," 46–53, and Survey Nos. 7–12, 26–28.

14. For the Virginia State Capitol, the national Capitol, and the University of Virginia Rotunda designs, see *Making of Virginia Architecture*, Survey Nos. 9–11 and 27. (By an error, the text for No. 11 does not make it clear that the newly discovered U.S. Capitol plan that had not even been photographed until 1990 is the upper figure on p. 219.) See also Richard Guy Wilson's Survey No. 67 on the enlargement of the Virginia Capitol in 1904–1905. In the face of self-serving attempts to relate Jefferson's proportional interests to the French avant-garde, Susan C. Riddick pointed out the genuine Palladian and Vitruvian lineage of Jefferson's cubic and spherical ideals in "The Influence of B. H. Latrobe on Jefferson's Design for the University of Virginia" (Master of Architectural History thesis, University of Virginia, 1988), 44–45.

15. See Brownell, *Making of Virginia Architecture*, esp. 49 and 79 n. 39.

16. The question of the two sets of drawings had puzzled writers ever since Kimball; see "Thomas Jefferson and the First Monument," 431–432. For the quotation from Clérisseau, see p.

604 in Clérisseau's account of expenditures (2 June 1786) in Boyd, *Jefferson Papers*, 9:603–604. See also fig. 40, p. 17, of this edition.

17. For the disclosure of the specifications, see Brien J. Poffenberger, "Jefferson's Design of the Capitol of Virginia" (Master of Architectural History thesis, University of Virginia, 1991). Marie Kimball's coverage appears in her work *Jefferson: The Scene of Europe, 1784 to 1789* (New York: Coward-McCann, 1950), 74 and 319 n. 69. The documents are in the collections of the Huntington Library, Art Collections, and Botanical Gardens, San Marino, Calif., Jefferson, T., "Notes explicatives des plans du Capitole pour l'état de la Virginie," 9 pp., N271, HM9374.

18. Quotation from "Notes explicatives," [1], as translated by Laurel Costa in Poffenberger, "Jefferson's Design," 65. See Clérisseau's *Antiquités de la France: Monumens de Nîmes* (Paris: de l'Imprimerie de Philippe-Denys Pierres, 1778), vii, for the statement that "artists and men of letters all agreed that Rome never had a more perfect monument than the *Maison quarrée*." I am indebted to Chantal Anne-Marie Maréchal, Associate Professor, Department of Foreign Languages, Virginia Commonwealth University, for assistance in translating the statement from the French.

19. I first proposed numbering the Jefferson conceptions as Designs 1, 2, and 3 for the exhibition "Jefferson and the Capitol of Virginia" at the Library of Virginia and at the DeWitt Wallace Decorative Arts Museum in Colonial Williamsburg in 2002–2003.

20. See Wilson, "Dating Jefferson's Early Architectural Drawings," *Virginia Magazine of History and Biography* 101 (Jan. 1993): 53–76 (esp. 56–60 dating the design ca. 1772 with revisions of 1780), and Wenger, "Thomas Jefferson and the Virginia State Capitol," ibid., 77–102 (esp. 81–86 favoring Jan.–Mar. 1776 as the date of preparation and Sept. or Oct. 1776 for the revisions).

21. On Jefferson's use of the Williamsburg plan for Richmond and on Wenger's place in the literature on Jefferson's architecture, see also pp. 322–323 n. 5, in Brownell, "Thomas Jefferson's Architectural Models and the United States Capitol," in *A Republic for the Ages: The United States Capitol and the Political Culture of the Early Republic*, ed. Donald R. Kennon (Charlottesville and London: Published for the United States Capitol Historical Society by the University Press of Virginia, 1999), 316–401. I differ from Wenger's symbolic interpretation of the Virginia Capitol. See also Wenger, "Jefferson's Designs for Remodeling the Governor's Palace," *Winterthur Portfolio* 32 (winter 1997): 223–242, esp. 232–234.

22. For comments on the "Temple Revival" that were compromised in editing, see Jeffrey A. Cohen and Charles E. Brownell, *The Architectural Drawings of Benjamin Henry Latrobe*, in *The Papers of Benjamin Henry Latrobe, Series 2, Architectural and*

Engineering Drawings, vol. 2 (New Haven: Yale University Press, for the Maryland Historical Society and the American Philosophical Society, 1994), esp. vol. 2, pt. 1, pp. 188, 190–193, 200, and vol. 2, pt. 2, pp. 359, 708, 711, 714–715. In 1915, when Kimball wrote his account of the impact of Jefferson's temple ("Thomas Jefferson and the First Monument," 485–491), he did not know of the second major temple-shaped building in the United States, Latrobe's Bank of Pennsylvania (Philadelphia, 1799–1801; demolished), an unsurpassed if indirect conduit for Jefferson's influence. It was Kimball, however, who rediscovered Latrobe's building. See Kimball, "The Bank of Pennsylvania, 1799: An Unknown Masterpiece of American Classicism," *Architectural Record* 44 (Aug. 1918): 132–139.

On my students' progress, see Brownell, "VCU's Sleuths and Thomas Jefferson's Virginia State Capitol," *Richmond Journal of History and Architecture* 1 (summer 1994): 3–7. Tending less to a revision of Kimball but making major disclosures about craftsmanship, Sumpter T. Priddy III and Martha C. Vick published "The Work of Clotworthy Stephenson, William Hodgson, and Henry Ingle in Richmond, Virginia, 1787–1806," *American Furniture* (1994): 206–233. The article offered important documentation about the activities of certain artisans at the Capitol, particularly Stephenson, a joiner, and Hodgson, a carver. One may respectfully decline to follow the attributions based on style and technique.

23. The McRoberts section has appeared posthumously in McRoberts's "Reconstruction of Jefferson's Rotunda in the Virginia Capitol," *Classicist*, no. 2 (1995–1996): 76, and in Brownell, "Jefferson's Architectural Models," fig. 8, p. 339; see also pp. 338–340 n. 16.

24. Saadat's work is "Jefferson, Palladio, Euhemerism, and the Virginia State Capitol" (Master of Arts thesis, Virginia Commonwealth University, 1994).

25. For Jefferson's characterization of the national Capitol, see Jefferson to Latrobe, 12 July 1812, in Latrobe, *The Papers of Benjamin Henry Latrobe*, ed. Thomas E. Jeffrey, microfiche edition (Clifton, N.J.: James T. White & Co. for the Maryland Historical Society, 1976), 209/E10. Jefferson actually called the Washington Capitol "the first temple dedicated to the sovereignty of the people." With the word *first* he presumably was not discounting his own Richmond Capitol as an earlier temple, but, more likely, was employing the word in another of its standard senses, "foremost in rank." One should keep in mind that, probably because of Jefferson's influence, the national Capitol was intended to have a templelike circular—"spherical"?—central room surrounding a white marble Washington statue or monument; see discussion later in this essay.

26. Joseph Senter White III, "Samuel Dobie, Thomas Jefferson, and the First Virginia Capitol in Richmond" (Master of Arts thesis,

Virginia Commonwealth University, 1997). For a more success-ful discussion of the vicissitudes of the Capitol roofing, see Robert B. Giles, "Lucky for Texas, Capitol's Lead Roof Leaked in 1790," *Richmond Journal of History and Architecture* 1 (summer 1994): 8. The representations of the second Williamsburg Capitol have not yet been analyzed properly. The problematic "E.R.D." view in fig. 21 of this essay shows the portico with upstairs pillars set over voids in a thoroughly unclassical fashion. The picture may record a state of the portico when supports had been added between the original columns of the upper level to reinforce a decaying structure.

27. The nature of the Richmond rotunda as an insertion into the design may account for why the room does not form a cube like its English models.

28. For Kimball's misunderstanding of the attic-podium issue, see "Thomas Jefferson and the First Monument," 474.

29. For the publication data on "Jefferson's Architectural Models," see n. 21 above. For Jefferson's letter to Latrobe of 12 June 1817, see B. Henry Latrobe, *The Correspondence and Miscellaneous Papers of Benjamin Henry Latrobe*, ed. John C. Van Horne et al., in *The Papers of Benjamin Henry Latrobe, Series 4, Correspondence and Miscellaneous Papers*, 3 vols. (New Haven: Yale University Press, for the Maryland Historical Society, 1984–1988), 3:901–903, and Latrobe, *Papers*, microfiche edition, 232/F3. Jefferson's "Notes explicatives," p. 4 (p. 70 in Poffenberger, as translated by Laurel Costa), sum up Jefferson's choices for Design 2 except for an Attic Order or Attic story: "The orders, Tuscan, Doric without mutules, Ionic with modil-lions, and Corinthian will be copied with the greatest exactitude from the first book of Palladio. The Ionic order with dentils will be copied from the temple of Fortuna Virilis of [that is, in] Palladio. The Doric order with mutules will be taken from such model as [Clérisseau] finds the best." The internal finale of Jefferson's selection was to be the rotunda, where Jefferson intended Palladio's Ionic under Palladio's Corinthian, or, rather, Leoni's adaptation of these two Orders in Palladio. The array of the Orders at the building as it stands in 2002 has not been prop-erly inventoried but is a mix ranging from Jeffersonian to very non-Jeffersonian choices.

30. First quotation from "Jefferson's Architectural Models," in *A Republic for the Ages*, 340. I am quoting Jefferson's expression "the time of the Caesars" from his letters to James Madison and to Edmund Randolph, 20 Sept. 1785 (Boyd, *Jefferson Papers*, 8:534–537, 537–539, [see esp. 535, 537]), and to James Buchanan and William Hay, 26 Jan. 1786 (ibid., 9:220–223 [quotation on 220]). For a different reading of the Virginia State Capitol, see 273–281 in Damie Stillman, "From the Ancient Roman Republic to the New American One: Architecture for a New Nation," in *A Republic for the Ages*, 271–315. Stillman attempts to argue for

the powerful influence of Roman Republican architecture in the Early Republic but rapidly has recourse to numerous Roman Imperial and other non-Republican sources. The article incorpo-rates the unpublished argument of John Stephens Crawford that Virginians, especially Samuel Dobie, reshaped the Richmond Capitol on the model of the Temple of Saturn in Rome, called the Temple of Concord by Palladio and other early writers. This is a misinterpretation that hinges on a drastic unfamiliarity with the Orders as used in seventeenth- and eighteenth-century Europe and a peculiar willingness to discount Jefferson's own statement that "I yielded, with reluctance, to . . . Clerissault, in his prefer-ence of the modern capital of Scamozzi to the more noble capital of antiquity." The misinterpretation, at least as reported by Stillman, also entails an implausible chronology for the Virginia Capitol. On Jefferson and "ancient" and "modern" Ionic capitals, see Brownell, Survey No. 10, in *Making of Virginia Architecture*. For an important investigation of Jefferson's values in relation to the Enlightenment, with some hard blows not only for the Republican fallacy but also for the notion that Jefferson sought a nationalistic architecture, see Kenneth Hafertepe, "An Inquiry into Thomas Jefferson's Ideas of Beauty," *Journal of the Society of Architectural Historians* 59 (June 2000): 216–231.

The Republican misinterpretation has a tie to the equally false notion that Jefferson was a Freemason and that a knowl-edge of Freemasonry will unlock the secrets of Jefferson's archi-tecture. There is no reason to think that Jefferson was a Mason. For a welcome corrective to the mythmaking about Freemasonry and architecture, see Melinda Byrd Frierson, "Freemasonry and Neo-Palladianism in Early Eighteenth-Century England" (Master of Architectural History thesis, University of Virginia, 1989).

31. In *Making of Virginia Architecture*, Survey No. 10, in a confes-sion of embarrassment, I referred to the Ionic entablature of the Fouquet model as having "somewhat unclear detail." The evolu-tion of the exterior Ionic Order of the Capitol is a major and problematic story. I hope that we shall see the puzzles resolved by Stanley R. Strong, Professor Emeritus of Psychology at Virginia Commonwealth University, who volunteered his expertise on the Orders to assist in the Colonial Williamsburg work on the Fouquet model. In 2002, three symposia and a book will expand our knowledge of Jefferson and the Capitol, and Virginia archi-tecture. The symposia, whose papers (as of this writing) will not be collected for publication, are "Palladio: From Rome to America" (sponsored by the Center for Palladian Studies in America) to be held in Richmond, 10 May 2002; "Jefferson and the Capitol of Virginia" celebrating the conservation of the Fouquet model (cosponsored by the Library of Virginia, the Colonial Williamsburg Foundation, the Center for Palladian Studies in America, and Virginia Commonwealth University), to be held in Williamsburg 27–28 Sept. 2002; and "Building Richmond," Virginia Commonwealth University's Tenth Annual Symposium in Architectural History (cosponsored by

the Virginia Historical Society, the Maymont Foundation, the Valentine Richmond History Center, the Center for Palladian Studies in America, the Library of Virginia, the Association for the Preservation of Virginia Antiquities, the Virginia Department of Historic Resources, and the Historic Richmond Foundation), to be held in Richmond on 11 Oct. 2002. Thanks to the encouragement of Tracy L. Kamerer, the Curator of State Art Collections at the Library of Virginia, particularly noteworthy papers at these conferences will be given by Virginia Commonwealth University graduate student Justin Gunther, who, as the present book goes to press, is completing a study of hundreds of Capitol construction documents that have been unknown to architectural historians as well as previously unnoticed emendations by Jefferson to his drawings and undetected sources for the Capitol design in Palladio and other sources. The book that will expand our knowledge, a long-awaited synthesis in three volumes, is *Architecture and Town Planning in Colonial North America* by James D. Kornwolf with the assistance of Georgiana W. Kornwolf (Baltimore, Md.: Johns Hopkins University Press), scheduled for publication in Nov. 2002.

INTRODUCTION TO THE 1989 EDITION

1. Kimball, "Thomas Jefferson and the First Monument of the Classical Revival in America," *Journal of the American Institute of Architects* 3 (Sept. 1915): 371–381; (Oct.): 421–433; (Nov.): 473–491. Kimball's scholarship entirely superseded the meager literature discussed in the initial paragraphs of his original monograph on the Capitol, and his critical review of that literature has been omitted from this third edition.

2. George Roberts and Mary Roberts, *Triumph on Fairmount: Fiske Kimball and the Philadelphia Museum of Art* (Philadelphia and New York: J. B. Lippincott, 1959), chap. 2, "Teaching and the Big Folio," 29–41; John Canaday, "Fiske Kimball," in *Culture Gulch: Notes on Art and Its Public in the 1960's* (New York: Farrar, Straus and Giroux, 1969), 139–143; obituary, *New York Times*, 16 Aug. 1955, p. 23, col. 3.

3. Dell Upton, "New Views of the Virginia Landscape," *Virginia Magazine of History and Biography* 96 (Oct. 1988): 405, 416, 425–427, 451–457; Mary Kane, *A Bibliography of the Works of Fiske Kimball*, ed. Frederick Doveton Nichols (Charlottesville: University of Virginia Press, 1959); Joseph Dye Lahendro, "Fiske Kimball: American Renaissance Historian" (Master of Architectural History thesis, University of Virginia, 1982); William B. O'Neal, "An Intelligent Interest in Architecture: A Bibliography of Publications about Thomas Jefferson as an Architect, Together with an Iconography of the Nineteenth-Century Prints of the University of Virginia," *Papers of the American Association of Architectural Bibliographers* 6 (1969): 3–150.

4. Marie Goebel Kimball, *Jefferson: The Road to Glory, 1743 to 1776* (New York: Coward-McCann, 1943), *Jefferson: War and Peace, 1776 to 1784* (New York: Coward-McCann, 1947), and *Jefferson: The Scene of Europe, 1784 to 1789* (New York: Coward-McCann, 1950).

5. Roberts and Roberts, *Triumph on Fairmount*, 30–34, 41; Frederick Doveton Nichols, Introduction, in Kimball, *Thomas Jefferson, Architect: Original Designs in the Coolidge Collection of the Massachusetts Historical Society* (Boston: Printed for Private Distribution at the Riverside Press, Cambridge, 1916, under the title *Thomas Jefferson, Architect: Original Designs in the Collection of Thomas Jefferson Coolidge, Junior*; reprint, New York: Da Capo Press, 1968), v–xi; Lahendro, "Fiske Kimball: American Renaissance Historian."

FISKE KIMBALL — THE CAPITOL OF VIRGINIA
A New Capitol

1. Julian P. Boyd et al., eds., *The Papers of Thomas Jefferson* (Princeton, N.J.: Princeton University Press, 1950–), 1:598–602 (hereafter cited as Boyd, *Jefferson Papers*).

2. William Waller Hening, ed., *The Statutes at Large: Being a Collection of All the Laws of Virginia, from the First Session of the Legislature, in the Year 1619* . . . (Richmond: Printed by and for Samuel Pleasants, Junior, Printer to the Commonwealth, 1809–1823), 10:85–89 (hereafter cited as Hening, *Statutes*).

3. Ibid., 10:85–89, 317–320.

4. Archibald Cary to Thomas Jefferson, 18 Dec. 1779, in Boyd, *Jefferson Papers*, 3:230; Hening, *Statutes*, 10:85–89, 317; 11:496; Fiske Kimball, "Jefferson and the Public Buildings of Virginia: II. Richmond, 1779–1780," *Huntington Library Quarterly* 12 (1948–1949): 303–310.

5. Hening, *Statutes*, 11:496. This Oct. 1784 statute also named Ambler and Hay as Directors to succeed Nicholas and Du Val.

6. Albert Ellery Bergh, ed., *The Writings of Thomas Jefferson* (Washington, D.C.: Issued under the Auspices of the Thomas Jefferson Memorial Association of the United States, 1903), 1:68–69.

7. Thomas Jefferson to James Madison, 1 Sept. 1785, in Boyd, *Jefferson Papers*, 8:462.

8. Thomas Jefferson to James Madison, 20 Sept. 1785, ibid., 8:534–535.

9. Thomas Jefferson to Edmund Randolph, 20 Sept. 1785, ibid., 8:537–538.

10. Bergh, *Writings of Thomas Jefferson*, 17:353–354. [ED. The 1989 edition of Kimball's work (p. 13) incorrectly omitted the word *on* in this passage.]

11. George Douglas to Thomas Jefferson, 15 Oct. 1800, Papers of Thomas Jefferson, 1606–1902, Series 1, General Correspondence, 1651–1827, 4 Jan. 1800–Feb. 1801, pp. 18417–18418 (images 515–517), microfilm and American Memory, Historical Collections for the National Digital Library online database, LC.

12. Thomas Jefferson to George Douglas, 21 Dec. 1800, ibid., p. 18517 (image 666). John Catanzariti and Eugene R. Sheridan of the *Papers of Thomas Jefferson* project graciously lent a copy of their draft transcript of this letter.

13. William Short to Thomas Jefferson, 28 July 1784, in Boyd, *Jefferson Papers*, 7:384–386.

14. James Buchanan and William Hay to Thomas Jefferson, 20 Mar. 1785, ibid., 8:48–49.

15. Thomas Jefferson to James Buchanan and William Hay, 13 Aug. 1785, ibid., 8:366–368.

16. James Buchanan and William Hay to Thomas Jefferson, 18 Oct. 1785, ibid., 8:648.

17. Thomas Jefferson to James Buchanan and William Hay, 26 Jan. 1786, ibid., 9:220–222. The recipients' given names were transposed in the heading to this printed text.

18. Thomas Jefferson to James Monroe, 27 Jan. 1786, ibid., 9:237.

19. Thomas Jefferson to James Buchanan and William Hay, 13 June 1786, ibid., 9:636.

20. Thomas Jefferson to James Buchanan and William Hay, 26 Dec. 1786, ibid., 10:632.

21. James Buchanan and William Hay to Thomas Jefferson, 18 Oct. 1785, ibid., 8:648; Thomas Jefferson to James Buchanan and William Hay, 13 Aug. 1785, ibid., 8:366.

22. Thomas Jefferson to James Buchanan and William Hay, 26 Jan. 1786, ibid., 9:220–221.

23. Jefferson Papers, Accounts and Clérisseau's Letter and Account, 9 Dec. 1789, Washington Statue and State Capitol Model, Records, 1786–1789, 1793, 1795–1796, 1802–1803, Auditor of Public Accounts, Inventory Entry No. 666, Library of Virginia, Richmond (hereafter cited as LVA). See also Boyd, *Jefferson Papers*, 9:603–604.

24. Jefferson Papers, Accounts and Clérisseau's Letter and Account, 9 Dec. 1789, Auditor of Public Accounts, Inventory Entry No. 666, LVA; translation by Linda J. Pike. A further entry in Jefferson's account with the commonwealth—"June 3, 1789, P[ai]d [Jean-Baptiste-Claude] Odiot for coffee pot as a present to Clérissault for his trouble with the drawings &c, of public buildings"—shows that Clérisseau's own personal services and advice were also handsomely acknowledged, but with a gift that only confirms the view of Clérisseau's limited advisory role. The coffeepot, or urn, is discussed and pictured in William Howard Adams, ed., *The Eye of Th[omas] Jefferson* (Washington, D.C.: National Gallery of Art, 1976), 306–307, and Boyd, *Jefferson Papers*, 15:xxvii–xxix, 172–173, 290. For scholarship on Clérisseau, see Thomas J. McCormick, "Charles-Louis Clérisseau," *Papers of the American Association of Architectural Bibliographers* 4 (1967): 9–16, and *Charles-Louis Clérisseau and the Genesis of Neo-Classicism* (New York: Architectural History Foundation; Cambridge, Mass., and London, Eng.: MIT Press, 1990).

25. Charles-Louis Clérisseau to Thomas Jefferson, 23 May 1797, Papers of Thomas Jefferson, Series 1, General Correspondence, 1651–1827, 4 Jan. 1794–13 June 1797, pp. 17395 [A–B] (images 1249–1250), LC; translation by Linda J. Pike.

FISKE KIMBALL — THE CAPITOL OF VIRGINIA
The Original Design

1. James Buchanan and William Hay to Thomas Jefferson, 20 Mar. and 18 Oct. 1785, in Julian P. Boyd et al., eds., *The Papers of Thomas Jefferson* (Princeton, N.J.: Princeton University Press, 1950–), 8:48–49, 648 (hereafter cited as Boyd, *Jefferson Papers*). Kimball's detailed description of these drawings and the hand-ruled papers on which Jefferson made them is omitted; he published a comprehensive discussion of these matters in his *Thomas Jefferson, Architect: Original Designs in the Collection of Thomas Jefferson Coolidge, Junior* (Boston: Printed for Private Distribution by the Riverside Press, Cambridge, 1916); reprinted under the title *Thomas Jefferson, Architect: Original Designs in the Coolidge Collection of the Massachusetts Historical Society*, with a new introduction by Frederick Doveton Nichols (New York: Da Capo Press, 1968).

2. Andrea Palladio's *I Quattro Libri dell'Architettura* was first published in Venice by Dominico de' Franceschi in 1570. Jefferson's ownership of several editions of Palladio's works is treated in E. Millicent Sowerby, comp., *Catalogue of the Library of Thomas Jefferson* (Washington, D.C.: Library of Congress,

1955; reprint, Charlottesville: University Press of Virginia, 1983), 4:359–364, and William Bainter O'Neal, *Jefferson's Fine Arts Library: His Selections for the University of Virginia Together with His Own Architectural Books* (Charlottesville: University Press of Virginia, 1976), 247–277. Influential in Jefferson's architectural work were Giacomo Leoni's editions of *The Architecture of A. Palladio; In Four Books*, ed. Giacomo Leoni and trans. Nicholas Dubois, 4 vols. in 5 (London: Printed by J[ohn] Watts, for the Author, 1715–1720); 2d ed., 2 vols. (London: Printed by John Darby for the Author, 1721); 3d ed., corrected, 1 vol. with notes and remarks of Inigo Jones, an appendix containing *The Antiquities of Rome*, written by A. Palladio, and *A Discourse of the Fires of the Ancients*, never before translated (London: Printed for A. Ward, S. Birt, D. Browne, C. Davis, T. Osborne, and A. Millar, 1742), and while in Paris he acquired a first edition of the French translation by Roland Fréart, sieur de Chambray, *Les Quatre Livres de l'Architecture d'Andre Palladio* (Paris: De l'Imprimerie d'Edme Martin, 1650).

3. Isaac Ware, ed., *The Four Books of Andrea Palladio's Architecture*, trans. Ware and Richard Boyle, third earl of Burlington, 4 vols. in 1. (London: I. Ware, 1738; reprinted as Andrea Palladio, *The Four Books of Architecture*, with a new introduction by Adolf K. Placzek, New York: Dover Publications, 1965), 27.

4. Jefferson Papers, Accounts for Duties and Transportation of Model, 9 Dec. 1789, Washington Statue and State Capitol Model, Records, 1786–1789, 1793, 1795–1796, 1802–1803, Auditor of Public Accounts, Inventory Entry No. 666, LVA; printed as "Instructions for Unpacking the Model of the Virginia Capitol, with Invoice," ca. 13 June 1786, in Boyd, *Jefferson Papers*, 9:637.

FISKE KIMBALL — THE CAPITOL OF VIRGINIA
Clérisseau's Drawings of Jefferson's Design

1. Thomas Jefferson to James Buchanan and William Hay, 26 Jan. 1786, in Julian P. Boyd et al., eds., *The Papers of Thomas Jefferson* (Princeton, N.J.: Princeton University Press, 1950–), 9:221 (hereafter cited as Boyd, *Jefferson Papers*). The sections to which Jefferson referred in this letter of transmission probably were never completed, for no item in payment for sections appears in any of the accounts; the Directors' letter reached Jefferson after he had sent the drawings and must have made him skeptical about the adoption of the plan.

2. Virginia Governor (1788–1791: Beverley Randolph), Executive Papers, 1788–1791, David Stuart to Gov. Beverley Randolph, 11 July 1791, Letters Received, 21 May–31 Aug. 1791, State

Government Records Collection, LVA (hereafter cited as Executive Papers, LVA).

3. Gov. Beverley Randolph to Dr. David Stuart, 25 July 1791, Secretary of the Commonwealth, Executive Letter Book 9, 1788–1792, Microfilm Reel 4, p. 231, LVA.

4. David Stuart to Gov. Beverley Randolph, 5 Aug. 1791. This letter was printed in William P. Palmer et al., eds., *Calendar of Virginia State Papers and Other Manuscripts Preserved in the Capitol at Richmond, 1652–1869* (Richmond: Rush U. Derr, Superintendent of Public Printing, 1875–1893), 5:356, from a manuscript then preserved at the Capitol, but it seems likely that the letter was not among the papers transferred to the Library of Virginia early in the twentieth century, for the archivists' thorough search of the relevant collections in 1988 and 2002 failed to locate the original.

5. William Hay to Gov. James Wood, 18 Mar. 1799, Letters Received, 1 Jan.–31 Mar. 1799, Executive Papers, 1796–1799, LVA.

6. James Dudley Morgan, "Maj. Pierre Charles L'Enfant, The Unhonored and Unrewarded Engineer," *Records of the Columbia Historical Society* 2 (1897–1898): 139–142. Kimball reported that the drawings of the Capitol of Virginia were not among L'Enfant's personal papers (then in the possession of James Dudley Morgan), at the Library of Congress, or at the office of the commissioner of public buildings and grounds. A sympathetic discussion of L'Enfant's dreams for the national capital noted, "At the same time that Pierre Charles L'Enfant was fired in Philadelphia, his quarters in the new federal city were burgled. His drawings, sketches, manuscripts, and books were taken to Francis Cabot's store, where his trunks were broken open. With the possible exception of a single drawing he never again saw his materials." J. L. Sibley Jennings Jr., "Artistry as Design: L'Enfant's Extraordinary City," *Quarterly Journal of the Library of Congress* 36 (1979): 244.

7. Jefferson Papers, Clérisseau's Letter and Account, 9 Dec. 1789, Washington Statue and State Capitol Model, Records, 1786–1789, 1793, 1795–1796, 1802–1803, Auditor of Public Accounts, Inventory Entry No. 666, LVA.

8. Writing on the eve of the Russian Revolution, Kimball stated in 1915 that his "letter addressed to the curator in Petrograd has brought no reply"; a 1986 letter to the director of the Hermitage Museum also brought no response. By 2002, however, the State Hermitage Museum had a Web site: http://www.hermitagemuseum.org/ (10 July 2002), and thumbnail prints of seventy-two of Clérisseau's drawings, none of them of Virginia's Capitol.

9. Thomas Jefferson to George Douglas, 21 Dec. 1800, Papers of Thomas Jefferson, 1606–1902, Series 1, General Correspondence,

1651–1827, 4 Jan. 1800–Feb. 1801, p. 18517 (image 666), micro-film and American Memory, Historical Collections for the National Digital Library online database, LC.

10. Thomas Jefferson to James Buchanan and William Hay, 26 Jan. 1786, in Boyd, *Jefferson Papers*, 9:220–222.

11. Albert Ellery Bergh, ed., *The Writings of Thomas Jefferson* (Washington, D.C.: Issued under the Auspices of the Thomas Jefferson Memorial Association of the United States, 1903), 1:68. Kimball was skeptical of the statement in Jefferson's memoir that he had adopted Clérisseau's suggestion that "the modern capital of [Vincenzo] Scamozzi" be substituted for the "more noble cap-ital of antiquity." Scamozzi's capital, with its four volutes placed diagonally on the corners, was indeed incorporated in the fin-ished building but added in Richmond well after Fouquet's model and the final drawings (later lost) had been sent from France. The columns of the plaster model have the antique Ionic capitals that Jefferson used elsewhere. Kimball reasoned that Jefferson would have mentioned any discrepancy between the model and the lost drawings in this respect. Because there is no mention of this in Jefferson's correspondence with the Directors, Kimball believed that the lost final drawings showed antique Ionic capitals like those of the model, and that in his recollection long after the event Jefferson was deceived by the change made during construction of the building.

12. Virginia Constitution of 1776, in William H. Gaines Jr., *Virginia History in Documents, 1621–1788* (Richmond: Virginia State Library, 1974), 68.

FISKE KIMBALL — THE CAPITOL OF VIRGINIA
"Finished with the Proper Ornaments"

1. Albert Ellery Bergh, ed., *The Writings of Thomas Jefferson* (Washington, D.C.: Issued under the Auspices of the Thomas Jefferson Memorial Association of the United States, 1903), 1:68.

2. Thomas Jefferson to William Short, 14 Dec. 1789, in Julian P. Boyd et al., eds., *The Papers of Thomas Jefferson* (Princeton, N.J.: Princeton University Press, 1950–), 16:26 (hereafter cited as Boyd, *Jefferson Papers*).

3. George Douglas to Thomas Jefferson, 15 Oct. 1800, Papers of Thomas Jefferson, 1606–1902, Series 1, General Correspondence, 1651–1827, 4 Jan. 1800–Feb. 1801, pp. 18417–18418 (images 515–517); George Douglas to Thomas Jefferson, 2 Aug. 1801, ibid., 26 June 1801–14 Nov. 1801, p. 19766 [A–B] (images 383–384), microfilm and American Memory, Historical Collections for the National Digital Library online database, LC.

4. Kimball's statement in the 1915 text that "the drawing men-tioned by Douglas . . . seems never to have been published" has been altered in light of the published engraving in a copy of *The Virginia & North Carolina Almanack for the Year 1802* (Petersburg: Published by Ross & Douglas, Booksellers and Stationers [1801]) in the Rare Book Collection of the Library of Virginia and the sup-porting evidence about Lawrence Sully (1769–1804) and Alexander Lawson (1773–1846) in George C. Groce and David H. Wallace, *The New-York Historical Society's Dictionary of Artists in America, 1564–1860* (New Haven, Conn.: Yale University Press, 1957), and Mantle Fielding, *Mantle Fielding's Dictionary of American Painters, Sculptors & Engravers*, ed. Glenn B. Opitz, 2d newly rev., enl., and updated ed. (Poughkeepsie, N.Y.: Apollo Book, 1986). For almanacs of the period see James A. Bear Jr. and Mary Caperton Bear, *A Checklist of Virginia Almanacs, 1732–1850* (Charlottesville: Bibliographical Society of the University of Virginia, 1962).

5. François Alexandre Frédéric, duc de La Rochefoucauld-Liancourt, *Travels through the United States of North America, the Country of the Iroquois, and Upper Canada, in the Years 1795, 1796, and 1797; with an Authentic Account of Lower Canada* (London: Printed for R. Phillips, 1799), 3:61.

6. Isaac Weld Jr., *Travels through the States of North America and the Provinces of Upper and Lower Canada, During the Years 1795, 1796, and 1797* (London: Printed for John Stockdale, 1799), 1:189–190.

7. Karl Bernhard, duke of Saxe-Weimar-Eisenach, *Travels through North America, during the Years 1825 and 1826* (Philadelphia: Carey, Lea, & Carey, 1828), 1:200.

8. Samuel Mordecai, *Richmond in By-Gone Days: Being Reminiscences of an Old Citizen* (Richmond: Published by George M. West, 1856), 58–59.

9. Capitol Square Data, Records, 1784–1931, Auditor of Public Accounts, Inventory Entry No. 655, LVA.

10. Albert Lybrock, Architectural Drawings and Plans, Virginia Capitol Building, 1858, Acc. 36480, General Architectural Files Collection, LVA.

11. Virginia Governor (1902–1906: Montague), Executive Papers, 1902–1906, Capitol Enlargement Correspondence, Bills, and Receipts, 1902–1906, Report of Capitol Enlargement Committee Submitted to Legislature, 24 Jan. 1906, Acc. 36710, State Government Records Collection, LVA (hereafter cited as Executive Papers, LVA).

12. John Kevan Peebles, Noland & Baskerville, Frye & Chesterman, Associated Architects, Architectural Drawings and Plans, Virginia State Capitol, 1904, 1904–1905, 1905, Acc. 36589, Drawings and Plans Collection, LVA.

13. *Richmond Virginia Gazette and Weekly Advertiser*, 20 Aug. 1785, p. 3, col. 1; James Buchanan and William Hay to Thomas Jefferson, 18 Oct. 1785, in Boyd, *Jefferson Papers*, 8:648.

14. Thomas Jefferson to James Madison, 8 Feb. 1786, ibid., 9:267.

15. James Madison to Thomas Jefferson, 18 Mar. 1786, ibid., 9:332.

16. Edmund Randolph to Thomas Jefferson, 12 July 1786, ibid., 10:133–134.

17. William Hay to Thomas Jefferson, 3 May 1787, ibid., 11:332–333.

18. Report of a Committee to Whom was Referred the Letter of the Directors of the Public Buildings, 14 Dec. 1789, Letters Received, Nov.–Dec. 1789, Executive Papers, 1789–1791, LVA.

19. William Hay to Gov. Beverley Randolph, 22 June 1790, Capitol Square Data, Records, 1784–1931, Correspondence, 1790, Auditor of Public Accounts, Inventory Entry No. 655, LVA.

20. Report of the Committee Regarding the Letter of the Directors of the Public Buildings, Enclosure with Robert Goode et al. to Gov. Henry Lee, 8 May 1792 (insert to letter dated 14 June 1792 from Robert Goode and William Hay), Letters Received, May–July 1792, Executive Papers, 1791–1794, LVA.

21. William Foushee to Gov. James Wood, 23 Oct. 1798, Letters Received, 21 Oct.–31 Oct. 1798, Executive Papers, 1796–1799, LVA.

22. John Clarke to Gov. James Monroe, 27 Jan. and 20 June 1801, Papers Respecting Arms, 1800–1802, Executive Papers, 1799–1802, LVA.

23. Michael B. Chesson, *Richmond After the War, 1865–1890* (Richmond: Virginia State Library, 1981), 114.

24. W. Asbury Christian, *Richmond: Her Past and Present* (Richmond: Manufactured by L. H. Jenkins, 1912), 320.

FISKE KIMBALL — THE CAPITOL OF VIRGINIA
Mr. Jefferson's Monument

1. Edmund Randolph to Thomas Jefferson, 12 July 1786, in Julian P. Boyd et al., eds., *The Papers of Thomas Jefferson* (Princeton, N.J.: Princeton University Press, 1950–), 10:133 (hereafter cited as Boyd, *Jefferson Papers*); Samuel Mordecai, *Richmond in By-Gone Days: Being Reminiscences of an Old Citizen* (Richmond: Published by George M. West, 1856), 87.

2. William Hay to Gov. Beverley Randolph, 11 May 1790, Capitol Square Data, Records, 1784–1931, Correspondence, 1790, Auditor of Public Accounts, Inventory Entry No. 655, LVA.

3. Virginia Governor (1794–1796: Robert Brooke), Executive Papers, 1794–1796, William Hay to Gov. Robert Brooke, 28 Nov. 1795, Letters Received, 21 Sept.–Nov. 1795, State Government Records Collection, LVA (hereafter cited as Executive Papers, LVA).

4. William Hay to Gov. James Wood, 9 Aug. 1798, Letters Received, July–Sept. 1798, Executive Papers, 1796–1799, LVA.

5. William Hay to Gov. Robert Brooke, 28 Nov. 1795, Letters Received, 21 Sept.–Nov. 1795, Executive Papers, 1794–1796, LVA.

6. *William and Mary Quarterly*, 1st ser., 11 (1902–1903): 270; 12 (1903–1904): 105; 20 (1911–1912): 22.

7. Samuel Dobie's Accounts with the Commonwealth of Virginia, Enclosure with William Hay to Gov. Robert Brooke, 28 Nov. 1795, Letters Received, 21 Sept.–Nov. 1795, Executive Papers, 1794–1796, LVA.

8. Enclosures with Robert Goode to Gov. Henry Lee, 14 June 1792, Letters Received, May–July 1792, Executive Papers, 1791–1794, LVA.

9. Talbot Faulkner Hamlin, *Benjamin Henry Latrobe* (New York: Oxford University Press, 1955); Paul F. Norton, comp., "Benjamin Henry Latrobe," *Papers of the American Association of Architectural Bibliographers* 9 (1972): 51–84.

10. Thomas Jefferson to James Buchanan and William Hay, 13 Aug. 1785, in Boyd, *Jefferson Papers*, 8:366–368.

REVEALING JEFFERSON'S MODEL FOR THE CAPITOL OF VIRGINIA

1. For additional analysis of the Fouquet model, its maker, its conservation, and its replication, see F. Carey Howlett, "Thomas Jefferson's Model for the Capitol of Virginia: A New Understanding," *Virginia Cavalcade* 51 (winter 2002): 4–15.

2. Thomas Jefferson to James Buchanan and William Hay, 26 Jan. 1786, Papers of Thomas Jefferson, 1606–1902, Series 1, General Correspondence, 1651–1827, 2 Jan. 1786–22 July 1786, pp. 3202–3205 (images 190–193), microfilm and American Memory, Historical Collections for the National Digital Library online database, LC.

3. Thomas Jefferson, "An Account of the Capitol in Virginia," 1785 [*sic*], Papers of Thomas Jefferson, ibid., 1 Aug.

1785–1785–90, pp. 2956–2957 (images 1007–1008), LC.

4. Fouquet's patron, the count Marie-Gabriel de Choiseul-Gouffier, was a wealthy aristocrat and diplomat. In 1782, he stimulated the French fascination for antiquity by publishing an account of his 1776 "voyage pittoresque" to Greece to document the ruins. Choiseul-Gouffier and his entourage may have been among the first to develop techniques for taking molds of classical sculpture and architectural features to fabricate full-size plaster replicas. In the 1780s, Choiseul-Gouffier commissioned Fouquet to produce a collection of models of the ancient temples of Greece and Italy. At the time, Fouquet apparently lived and worked on the premises of the count's Hôtel de Gouffier, in Paris, which is probably where he made the model of the Virginia Capitol.

5. Most of the models by Fouquet, and the entire later body of work by his son François, were miniature replicas of buildings from antiquity. Early in Fouquet's career, these formed prized collections owned by wealthy amateur enthusiasts of classical architecture such as Choiseul-Gouffier, whose collection was confiscated during the French Revolution of 1789–1799. The revolutionaries, including Fouquet, deposited the items in the Louvre with the intent of creating a museum of architecture. The museum never came to pass, and Choiseul-Gouffier eventually returned to Paris and reclaimed his models. He apparently employed Fouquet and his son to build additional ones, which were installed in a Paris gallery early in the nineteenth century.

Classical architecture took on new significance during and after the French Revolution, with scholarly revolutionaries such as Louis-François Cassas calling for a new architecture drawing on noble ancient sources. Cassas became Fouquet's most important patron and advocate early in the nineteenth century, establishing his own gallery featuring models of ancient architecture. Although the gallery contained models by a number of artists, Jacques-Guillaume Legrand, the renowned French architect of public monuments, pointed out that "the best made ones are due to the very distinguished talents of M. Fouquet, architectural modelmaker, and that he has achieved perfection concerning correct proportions and precision in forms."

In later years, Fouquet's work drew the attention of noted British collectors and architects such as John Nash, who purchased fifteen models in 1820, and Sir John Soane, who bought twenty (by François Fouquet and on a smaller scale, 1:128) in 1834. The Victoria and Albert Museum, in London, eventually acquired Nash's collection. The collections at the Victoria and Albert and at Sir John Soane's Museum, also in London, survive. Of the other extant models, perhaps the most important for purposes of comparison with the Capitol model are three bridge models at the Musée Carnavalet, in Paris. Probably made in 1788, these are the only surviving Fouquet works reliably dating from the same period as Jefferson's Capitol model.

The author thanks the following for information and assistance in examining Fouquet models: Fiona Leslie, Marjorie Trusted, James Yorke, Sasha Kosinova, and Mererid Roberts at the Victoria and Albert Museum; Helen Dorey at Sir John Soane's Museum; and Renee Davray-Piekolek at the Musée Carnavalet. Geneviève Cuisset generously shared her groundbreaking research, including unpublished information, on the work of Jean-Pierre and François Fouquet, and Werner Szambien provided useful insight into the work of Charles-Louis Clérisseau and the Fouquets within the context of eighteenth-century French Neoclassicism. The author also thanks Olivia Eller and Chris Augerson for researching French texts and providing excellent translations of pertinent passages.

See Geneviève Cuisset, "Jean-Pierre et François Fouquet, Artistes Modeleurs," *Gazette des Beaux-Arts*, 6 period, vol. 115 (May–June 1990): 227–240, and Werner Szambien, *Le Musée d'Architecture* (Paris: Picard, 1988).

6. Jean-Pierre Fouquet, "Observations essentielle pour deballer le modelle," ca. 13 June 1786, Jefferson Papers, Accounts for Duties and Transportation of Model, 9 Dec. 1789, Washington Statue and State Capitol Model, Records, 1786–1789, 1793, 1795–1796, 1802–1803, Auditor of Public Accounts, Inventory Entry No. 666, LVA; printed as "Instructions for Unpacking the Model of the Virginia Capitol, with Invoice," ca. 13 June 1786, in *The Papers of Thomas Jefferson*, ed. Julian P. Boyd et al. (Princeton, N.J.: Princeton University Press, 1950–), 9:637.

7. Account, Philip Sturtevant for repairing model of the Capitol, 17 Oct. 1829, and Account, C. W. McGinness and Philip Sturtevant for painting and repairing model, 12 June 1834, Capitol Square Data, Records, 1784–1931, Auditor of Public Accounts, Inventory Entry No. 655, LVA. The author thanks Tracy Kamerer and Barbara Batson of the Library of Virginia for providing these documents.

8. The group included the Honorable Susan Clark Schaar, Clerk of the Senate; the Honorable Bruce Jamerson, Clerk of the House of Delegates; the Library staff members responsible for the model (Tracy Kamerer, Curator of State Art Collections, Audrey Johnson, Senior Specialist for Picture Collections, Selden Richardson, Architectural Plans and Drawings Archivist, and Conley Edwards, State Archivist); three prominent architectural historians noted for their study of Jefferson's architecture: William Beiswanger of The Thomas Jefferson Memorial Foundation, Charles Brownell of Virginia Commonwealth University, and Murray Howard of the University of Virginia; and the author. Charles Brownell later joined with Library staff members, including Kip Campbell, Tom Camden, Tracy Kamerer, Selden Richardson, and Barbara Batson, to oversee the conservation project. The author thanks all of these individuals for their contributions, with special appreciation to Tracy Kamerer for enthusiastically monitoring

the progress of the project, for tirelessly researching pertinent documents, and for suggesting further avenues for investigation; to Barbara Batson for her many hours of outstanding work coordinating the exhibition "Jefferson and the Capitol of Virginia"; and to Charles Brownell for providing invaluable insight into Jefferson's architecture and the Capitol design that informed the entire project.

9. See Cuisset, "Jean-Pierre et François Fouquet, Artistes Modeleurs," 227–240.

10. The inventory is on deposit at the French National Archives (Archive Nationales—Musée de l'Histoire de France), XLVI–836.14, MC (15 June 1829), Paris, France. The author thanks Geneviève Cuisset for providing transcriptions and Olivia Eller for translating them.

11. Project conservator Amy Fernandez discovered the simulated ashlar as well as the dark-painted-paper window inserts, which also bore painted mullions, during her painstaking examination and conservation treatment of the model. Pamela Young, paper conservator, identified the composition and approximate age of the paper.

12. The author thanks John Watson for preparing outstanding drawings of the Capitol model and for assuming direction of the complex project to reproduce the model following the author's departure from Colonial Williamsburg. Thanks also to Colonial Williamsburg staff members Chris Swan, Albert Skutans, Tom Snyder, and volunteer John Piazza for their skill and dedication in fabricating and assembling the reproduction, and to contractors Gary Lavarack and Joseph Hutchins for special expertise in fabricating some of the detailed elements. The author also thanks the Roland Corporation for the generous loan of two scanning and milling machines used to make the reproduction. Mark Wenger, architectural historian at Colonial Williamsburg, and Stanley Strong, professor emeritus at Virginia Commonwealth University, contributed to the interpretation of the X-radiographs. Owen Howlett assisted with the research of design prototypes.

13. James Gibbs, *Rules for Drawing the Several Parts of Architecture* (London: Printed by W. Bowyer for the Author, 1732; republished in 1968 as *Rules for Drawing* by Gregg International Publishers, Farnborough, Hants., England), 33–34, Plates 46 and 47; Jefferson owned this book as early as 1769 (for the architectural books owned by Jefferson, see William Bainter O'Neal, *Jefferson's Fine Arts Library: His Selections for the University of Virginia Together with His Own Architectural Books* [Charlottesville: University Press of Virginia, 1976]). See console from Vincenzo Scamozzi, *L'Idea dell'Architettura Universale* (Venice: Expensis Auctoris, 1615), in Alexander Tzonis and Liane Lefaivre, *Classical*

Architecture: The Poetics of Order (Cambridge, Mass.: MIT Press, 1986), 82.

14. Thanks to Charles Brownell for noting Jefferson's intentional juxtaposition of ornamented and plain friezes at the University of Virginia.

15. It is curious that the builders of the Capitol, apparently unguided by Jefferson or Clérisseau, returned to the Maison Carrée for the design of the small coffers ornamenting the bottom surfaces of the entablature beams. According to nineteenth-century images, the larger expanse of the original portico ceiling was flat. This was replaced by a simplified version of the Maison Carrée coffered ceiling during the 1904–1906 renovation.

16. Andrea Palladio, *The Architecture of A. Palladio; In Four Books*, 2d ed., 2 vols. (London: Printed by John Darby for the Author, 1721), Book 1, Chap. 23, pp. 39–40. Dimensions for the length (340.98 mm), breadth (128.67 mm) and height (239.45mm) of the portico interior were determined from X-ray images by John Watson. The dimensions for length and breadth were measured from the bottom inner edges of the entablature beams, with .88 mm (the amount the bottom edge of the entablature beam projects from the facade wall) added on all four sides to give imaginary "wall to wall" dimensions. According to Palladio's rule, the ceiling height is calculated as follows: 340.98 (L) plus 128.67 (W) = 469.65 / 2 = 234.83mm, which varies less than 2 percent from the actual measured height of 239.45mm. Palladio's disciple Scamozzi utilized the same rule in his *L'Idea dell'Architettura Universale* (Venice, 1615), according to chamber proportions evident in a plate reproduced in Tzonis and Lefaivre, *Classical Architecture: The Poetics of Order*, 92. This plate was apparently the source for Plate 54 in Gibbs's *Rules for Drawing the Several Parts of Architecture,* which shows ceilings with marked similarity to that of the model. Gibbs also expressed Palladio's rule for determining the height of rooms with coved ceilings more concisely than the master: "let the length and breadth of them be added together, half the sum is the height of the Room"(p. 37).

17. Palladio, *The Architecture of A. Palladio; In Four Books*, Book 1, Chap. 16, p. 26.

18. "Notes explicatives des plans du Capitole pour l'état de la Virginie," 9 pp., N271, HM9374, Thomas Jefferson, 1785, Huntington Library, Art Collections, and Botanical Gardens, San Marino, Calif.; translation by Laurel Costa in Brien J. Poffenberger, "Jefferson's Design of the Capitol of Virginia" (Master of Architectural History thesis, University of Virginia, 1991). Calculating from the dimensions Jefferson provided in his "Notes" (9′1″ between columns and a column diameter of 4′2″), one finds his exact proposed intercolumniation to be 2.18. Like that of the Capitol model, it is a bit less than Palladio's ideal

Eustyle spacing. Interestingly, Jefferson's final portico elevation (Massachusetts Historical Society: K116/N279) exhibits an intercolumniation of exactly 2¼ modules. He achieved this by narrowing the diameter of five of the columns, making them 9.37 modules high. The slightly wider column on the far right, meanwhile, at 8.82 modules, is nearly identical to those on Fouquet's model, and may illustrate his actual desired column proportion (the use of wider columns obviously reduces the intercolumniation, which may explain Jefferson's description of his column spacing as "approximately the Eustyle"). Although much of the design put forth in the "Notes" was discarded after Jefferson met Clérisseau, it is clear from his final portico elevation and from Fouquet's model that the important proportional relationships of Jefferson's Palladian Ionic exterior survived. The author thanks Stanley Strong for suggesting an investigation of the relationship between Palladio's Ionic order and that on the Capitol model.

19. In his "Notes explicative" Jefferson proposed, in addition to other models, copying the Ionic order from Palladio's Fortuna Virilis for the Capitol interior (see Poffenberger), so it is not surprising to find elements of it on the model's exterior. These elements include the capitals, with outermost volutes oriented diagonally on the corner columns, and the architrave, with an ornamented cyma reversa and bead-and-reel molding below the uppermost fascia (see Plate 37, Book 4 of Leoni's *Architecture of A. Palladio*). Meanwhile, the temple's column proportions (9.17 modules) and spacing (1.94 modules) were ignored in favor of Palladio's ideal Ionic order. See also Charles Brownell's discussion of the Ionic capitals on the model in comparison to the "modern" ones on the Capitol building (*The Making of Virginia Architecture* [Richmond: Virginia Museum of Fine Arts, 1992], Survey 10).

20. Thomas Jefferson to James Madison, 1 Sept. 1785, in Boyd, *Jefferson Papers*, 8:462.

21. Thomas Jefferson to James Madison, 8 Feb. 1786, Papers of Thomas Jefferson, Series 1, General Correspondence, 1651–1827, 2 Jan. 1786–22 July 1786, pp. 3251–3256 (images 258–263), LC.

EPIOLOGUE
An Intelligent Regard to the Model

1. *Journal of the House of Delegates of Virginia, for the Session of 1849–50* (Richmond: William F. Ritchie, Public Printer, 1849), 91, 125, 134, 157, 376, 381; "Report of the Superintendent of Public Edifices, 1855–6 & 1856–7," Doc. No. 24, p. 3, supplement to *Journal of the House of Delegates*, 1857–1858 sess.; Karen Lang Kummer, "The Evolution of the Virginia State Capitol, 1779–1965" (Master of Architectural History thesis, University of Virginia, 1981), 26–27.

2. Kummer, "The Evolution of the Virginia State Capitol," 26–28; John E. Wells and Robert E. Dalton, *The Virginia Architects, 1835–1955: A Biographical Dictionary* (Richmond: New South Architectural Press, 1997), 270–271; Calder Loth, ed., *The Virginia Landmarks Register*, 4th ed. (Charlottesville: University Press of Virginia, 1999), 435; L. Moody Simms Jr., "Seven Architects of Nineteenth-Century Richmond," *Virginia Record* 100 (Nov. 1978): 19, 66; Letter of Samuel Chilton, Richmond, to the Secretary of War, Confederate States of America, 23 Oct. 1862, in Compiled Service Records of Confederate Soldiers Who Served in Organizations from the State of Virginia, Fifteenth Infantry, Le–Mi, National Archives and Records Administration, Washington, D.C.; "The Hand of Death," *Richmond Dispatch*, 12 Jan. 1886, p. 1; Mary H. Mitchell, *Hollywood Cemetery: The History of a Southern Shrine* (Richmond: Virginia State Library, 1985; reprint, Richmond: Library of Virginia, 1999), 44. The estimated cost of Lybrock's proposed remodeling of the Capitol was $46,210. *Journal of the House of Delegates of . . . Virginia, for the Session of 1857–58* (Richmond: William F. Ritchie, Public Printer, 1857), 272.

3. Albert Lybrock, Architectural Drawings and Plans, Virginia Capitol Building, 1858, Acc. 36480, General Architectural Files Collection, LVA.

4. Blair Bolling, "Report of the Superintendent of Public Edifices," Doc. 1, p. 81, in *Journal of the House of Delegates of the Commonwealth of Virginia . . . December [1834]* (Richmond: Printed by Thomas Ritchie, Printer to the Commonwealth, 1834); Gov. Henry A. Wise, "Message III, on Miscellaneous Subjects, to the General Assembly of Virginia, December 7, 1857," Doc. No. 1, p. 155, supplement to *Journal of the House of Delegates*, 1857–1858 sess.; Kummer, "Evolution of the Virginia State Capitol, "26–29; *Richmond Whig*, 28–30 Apr. 1870; *A Full Account of the Great Calamity, Which Occurred in the Capitol at Richmond, Virginia, April 27, 1870, Together with a List of Killed and Wounded* (Richmond: Ellyson & Taylor, 1870); "The Richmond Calamity," *Harper's Weekly*, 14 May 1870; George L. Christian, *The Capitol Disaster: A Chapter of Reconstruction in Virginia* (Richmond: Richmond Press, 1915), 24–30; Michael B. Chesson, *Richmond After the War, 1865–1890* (Richmond: Virginia State Library, 1981), 187–188; [Edward D. C. Campbell, Jr.], "Capitol Prospects: Two Views of the Virginia Capitol," *Virginia Cavalcade* 43 (autumn 1993): 72.

5. Sherwin McRae's pamphlet, *Virginia State Capitol: An Historical Account of the Erection of the Capitol, and the Review of the Question of Its Preservation* (Richmond: N.p., 1871) (quotation on 2), first appeared in the *Old Dominion Magazine*, 15 Aug. 1871 (quotation on 484).

6. *Journal of the Senate of the Commonwealth of Virginia Begun . . . December 4, 1901* (Richmond: J. H. O'Bannon, Superintendent of

Public Printing, 1901), 29; Kummer, "Evolution of the Virginia State Capitol," 30.

7. *Journal of the Senate* (1901), 150; Kummer, "Evolution of the Virginia State Capitol," 30; *Acts and Joint Resolutions Passed by the General Assembly of . . . Virginia, During the Session of 1901–2* (Richmond: J. H. O'Bannon, Superintendent of Public Printing, 1902), 465–466.

8. *Acts of Assembly* (1901–1902), 465; Kummer, "Evolution of the Virginia State Capitol," 31–32, 34–36; Virginia Governor (1902–1906: Montague), Executive Papers, 1902–1906, Capitol Enlargement Correspondence, Bills, and Receipts, 1902–1906, Minutes of the Capitol Building Commission, Acc. 36710, State Government Records Collection, LVA (hereafter cited as Executive Papers, LVA). The commission consisted of the governor and five members of the General Assembly, three from the House of Delegates and two from the Senate. Its last meeting was held on 12 Nov. 1903, when it adjourned "to meet subject to call of chairman."

9. *Journal of the Senate of . . . Virginia Begun . . . January 13, 1904* (Richmond: J. H. O'Bannon, Superintendent of Public Printing, 1904), 18; *Acts and Joint Resolutions Passed by the General Assembly of the State of Virginia, During the Session of 1904* (Richmond: J. H. O'Bannon, Superintendent of Public Printing, 1904), chap. 62, p. 108 (this act also rescinded the appropriation of $100,000 for renovation of the Capitol that had been passed in Apr. 1902 and reconstituted the Capitol Building Commission with three members from each house including three holdovers from the previous commission); *Journal of the Senate of . . . Virginia Begun . . . January 10, 1906* (Richmond: Davis Bottom, Superintendent of Public Printing, 1906); *Specifications for Fire Proofing and Additions to the Virginia State Capitol, Richmond, Va.*, Capitol Enlargement Correspondence, Executive Papers, 1902–1906, LVA; Kummer, "Evolution of the Virginia State Capitol," 36–38.

10. Kummer, "Evolution of the Virginia State Capitol," 38–39, 50; *Richmond Dispatch*, 14 Dec. 1902.

11. Kummer, "Evolution of the Virginia State Capitol," 37–40; "Report of the Committee on the Enlargement, Restoration and Repair of the Capitol," 24 Jan. 1906, Doc. No. 3, p. 4, *Journal of the Senate* (1906).

12. *Acts and Joint Resolutions . . . of the General Assembly of . . . Virginia . . . January 13, 1926* (Richmond: Davis Bottom, Superintendent of Public Printing, 1926), chap. 334, p. 601; *Acts and Joint Resolutions . . . of the General Assembly of . . . Virginia . . . March 16, 1927* (Richmond: Davis Bottom, Superintendent of Public Printing, 1927), chap. 72, p. 166; Kummer, "Evolution of the Virginia State Capitol," 41–42; *Richmond Enquirer*, 4 Aug. 1807; E. Griffith Dodson, *The Capitol of the Commonwealth of Virginia at Richmond: Portraits, Statuary, Inscriptions, and Biographical Sketches* (Richmond: N.p., 1937), 23, 29, 33–34.

13. Warren Strother, "Restoring the Capitol: Behind Mr. Jefferson's 1785 Walls, an Interior for 1964," *Commonwealth* 30 (Feb. 1963): 22–25; Kummer, "Evolution of the Virginia State Capitol," 43–45; R. N. Anderson Jr., "The Commonwealth's Capitol," *Virginia Record* 84 (Jan. 1964): 27–29.

14. *Acts of the General Assembly of . . . Virginia, 1999 . . . Reconvened [Session]* (Richmond: N.p., 1999), chap. 976, pp. 2583–2585.

15. Albert Matthews, ed., "Journal of William Loughton Smith, 1790–1791," *Proceedings of the Massachusetts Historical Society* 51 (1917–1918): 65–66.

Selected Bibliography

Adams, William Howard, ed. *The Eye of Th[omas] Jefferson.* Exhibition catalog. Washington, D.C.: National Gallery of Art, 1976.

Alexander, Robert L. "Maximilian Godefroy in Virginia: A French Interlude in Richmond's Architecture." *Virginia Magazine of History and Biography* 69 (Oct. 1961): 420–431.

————. *The Architecture of Maximillian Godefroy.* Baltimore and London: Johns Hopkins University Press, 1974.

Anderson, R. N., Jr. "The Commonwealth's Capitol." *Virginia Record* 84 (Jan. 1964): 27–29.

Barnett, Elizabeth J. "John Clarke (1766–1844), Richmond Architect and Industrialist." Master of Arts thesis, Virginia Commonwealth University, 2001.

Bergh, Albert Ellery, ed. *The Writings of Thomas Jefferson.* 20 vols. Washington, D.C.: Issued under the Auspices of the Thomas Jefferson Memorial Association of the United States, 1903.

Boyd, Julian P., et al., eds. *The Papers of Thomas Jefferson.* 29 vols. to date. Princeton, N.J.: Princeton University Press, 1950– .

Bricker, Lauren Weiss. "American Backgrounds: Fiske Kimball's Study of Architecture in the United States." In *The Early Years of Art History in the United States: Notes and Essays on Departments, Teaching, and Scholars.* Edited by Craig Hugh Smyth and Peter M. Lukehart. Princeton, N.J.: Department of Art and Archaeology, Princeton University, 1993.

————. "The Contributions of Fiske Kimball and Talbot Faulkner Hamlin to the Study of American Architectural History." Ph. D. diss., University of California, Santa Barbara, 1992.

————. "Kimball, Fiske." *American National Biography.* Edited by John A. Garraty and Mark C. Carnes. 24 vols. New York: Oxford University Press, 1999, 12:675–676.

————. "The Writings of Fiske Kimball: A Synthesis of Architectural History and Practice." In *The Architectural Historian in America*, Studies in the History of Art, 35, Center for Advanced Study in the Visual Arts, Symposium Papers 19. Series editor Elisabeth Blair MacDougall. Washington, D.C.: National Gallery of Art, 1990.

Brownell, Charles E. "Thomas Jefferson's Architectural Models and the United States Capitol." In *A Republic for the Ages: The United States Capitol and the Political Culture of the Early Republic.* Edited by Donald R. Kennon. Charlottesville and London: Published for the United States Capitol Historical Society by the University Press of Virginia, 1999.

————. "VCU's Sleuths and Thomas Jefferson's Virginia State Capitol." *Richmond Journal of History and Architecture* 1 (summer 1994): 3–7.

————; Calder Loth; William M. S. Rasmussen; and Richard Guy Wilson. *The Making of Virginia Architecture.* Richmond: Virginia Museum of Fine Arts, 1992.

[Campbell, Edward D. C., Jr.]. "Capitol Prospects: Two Views of the Virginia Capitol." *Virginia Cavalcade* 43 (autumn 1993): 70–73.

[————]. "The Reviewing Stand." *Virginia Cavalcade* 38 (winter 1989): [98].

Canaday, John. *Culture Gulch: Notes on Art and Its Public in the 1960's.* New York: Farrar, Straus and Giroux, 1969.

Capitol Enlargement Committee, Records, 1904–1906. Virginia General Assembly. Acc. 30171. State Government Records Collection, Library of Virginia.

Capitol Enlargement Correspondence, Bills, and Receipts, 1902–1906. Virginia Governor (1902–1906: Montague), Executive Papers. Acc. 36710. State Government Records Collection, Library of Virginia.

Capitol Square Data, Records, 1784–1931. Auditor of Public Accounts, Inventory Entry No. 655, Library of Virginia.

Carter, Edward C., II; John C. Van Horne; and Charles E. Brownell, eds. *Latrobe's View of America, 1795–1820: Selections from the Watercolors and Sketches.* In *Papers of Benjamin Henry Latrobe: Series 3, The Sketchbooks and Miscellaneous Drawings.* New Haven: Published for the Maryland Historical Society by Yale University Press, 1985.

Chesson, Michael B. *Richmond After the War, 1865–1890.* Richmond: Virginia State Library, 1981.

Christian, George L. *The Capitol Disaster: A Chapter of Reconstruction in Virginia*. Richmond: Richmond Press, 1915.

Christian, W. Asbury. *Richmond: Her Past and Present*. Richmond: Manufactured by L. H. Jenkins, 1912.

Clérisseau, Charles-Louis. *Antiquités de la France: Monumens de Nîmes*. Paris: de l'Imprimerie de Philippe-Denys Pierres, 1778.

Cohen, Jeffrey A., and Charles E. Brownell. *The Architectural Drawings of Benjamin Henry Latrobe*. In *The Papers of Benjamin Henry Latrobe*, Series 2, Architectural and Engineering Drawings. Vol. 2. New Haven: Yale University Press, for the Maryland Historical Society and the American Philosophical Society, 1994.

Cuisset, Geneviève. "Jean-Pierre et François Fouquet, Artistes Modeleurs." *Gazette des Beaux-Arts*, 6 period, vol. 115 (May–June 1990): 227–240.

Dessypris, Mary, and Jennifer Davis McDaid. *The Virginia Capitol: An American Architectural Milestone*. Pamphlet. Records and Resources at the Library of Virginia. Richmond, Nov. 2001.

Dodson, E. Griffith. *The Capitol of the Commonwealth of Virginia at Richmond: Portraits, Statuary, Inscriptions, and Biographical Sketches*. Richmond: N.p., 1937.

Frary, I. T. *Thomas Jefferson, Architect and Builder*. With an Introduction by Fiske Kimball. Richmond: Garrett and Massie, 1931. 3d ed. Richmond: Garrett and Massie, 1950.

Frierson, Melinda Byrd. "Freemasonry and Neo-Palladianism in Early Eighteenth-Century England." Master of Architectural History thesis, University of Virginia, 1989.

A Full Account of the Great Calamity, Which Occurred in the Capitol at Richmond, Virginia, April 27, 1870, Together with a List of Killed and Wounded. Richmond: Ellyson and Taylor, 1870.

Giles, Robert B. "Lucky for Texas, Capitol's Lead Roof Leaked in 1790." *Richmond Journal of History and Architecture* 1 (summer 1994): 8.

Guinness, Desmond, and Julius Trousdale Sadler Jr. *Mr. Jefferson, Architect*. New York: Viking Press, 1973.

Hafertepe, Kenneth. "An Inquiry into Thomas Jefferson's Ideas of Beauty." *Journal of the Society of Architectural Historians* 59 (June 2000): 216–231.

Hening, William Waller, ed. *The Statutes at Large: Being a Collection of All the Laws of Virginia, from the First Session of the Legislature in the Year 1619. . . .* 13 vols. Richmond: Printed by and for Samuel Pleasants, Junior, Printer to the Commonwealth; New York and Philadelphia, 1809–1823.

Historic American Buildings Survey. Virginia State Capitol, Richmond, Va. Survey No. VA 1254. Washington, D.C.: National Park Service, Summer 1988. Historic American Buildings Survey, HABS, VA, 44-RICH, 9-, American Memory, Historical Collections for the National Digital Library online database, Prints and Photographs Division, Library of Congress, Washington, D.C.

Hitchcock, Henry-Russell, and William Seale. *Temples of Democracy: The State Capitols of the U.S.A.* New York: Harcourt Brace Jovanovich, 1976.

Howlett, F. Carey. "Thomas Jefferson's Model for the Capitol of Virginia: A New Understanding." *Virginia Cavalcade* 51 (winter 2002): 4–15.

Jefferson, Thomas. "An Account of the Capitol in Virginia." In Papers of Thomas Jefferson, 1785 [*sic*], Series 1, General Correspondence, 1651–1827, 1 Aug. 1785–1785–90, pp. 2956–2957 (images 1007–1008), microfilm and American Memory, Historical Collections for the National Digital Library online database, Library of Congress, Manuscript Division, Washington, D.C.

———. "Notes explicatives des plans du Capitole pour l'état de la Virginie," N271, HM9374, Huntington Library, San Marino, Calif.

———. Papers, 1606–1902, Series 1, General Correspondence, 1651–1827, microfilm and American Memory, Historical Collections for the National Digital Library online database, Library of Congress, Manuscript Division, Washington, D.C.

———. *Thomas Jefferson's Library: A Catalog with the Entries in His Own Order*. Edited by James Gilreath and Douglas L. Wilson. Washington, D.C.: Library of Congress, 1989.

Kalbian, Maral S. "The Ionic Order and the Progression of the Orders in American Palladianism before 1812." Master of Architectural History thesis, University of Virginia, 1988.

Kane, Mary. *A Bibliography of the Works of Fiske Kimball*. Edited by Frederick Doveton Nichols. Charlottesville: University of Virginia Press, 1959.

Kimball, Fiske. "The Bank of Pennsylvania, 1799: An Unknown Masterpiece of American Classicism." *Architectural Record* 44 (Aug. 1918): 132–139.

———. "Jefferson and the Public Buildings of Virginia: I. Williamsburg, 1770–1776." *Huntington Library Quarterly* 12 (1948–1949): 115–120.

———. "Jefferson and the Public Buildings of Virginia: II. Richmond, 1779–1780." *Huntington Library Quarterly* 12 (May 1949): 303–310.

———. "Thomas Jefferson and the First Monument of the Classical Revival in America." *Journal of the American Institute of Architects* 3 (Sept. 1915): 371–381; (Oct.): 421–433; (Nov.): 473–491.

———. "Thomas Jefferson and the First Monument of the Classical Revival in America." Ph.D. dissertation, University of Michigan, 1915.

———. "Thomas Jefferson and the Origins of the Classical Revival in America." *Art and Archaeology* 1 (1915): 218–227.

———. *Thomas Jefferson, Architect: Original Designs in the Collection of Thomas Jefferson Coolidge, Junior*. Boston: Printed for Private Distribution by the Riverside Press, Cambridge, 1916. Reprinted under the title *Thomas Jefferson, Architect: Original Designs in the Coolidge Collection of the Massachusetts Historical Society*, with a new introduction by Frederick Doveton Nichols. New York: Da Capo Press, 1968.

Kimball, Marie. *Jefferson: The Scene of Europe, 1784 to 1789*. New York: Coward-McCann, 1950.

[Kukla, Jon]. "'Beformed on a study of antient models': Virginia's Capitol Is America's First Monument of the Classic Revival." *Virginia Cavalcade* 29 (spring 1980): 148–149.

Kummer, Karen Lang. "The Evolution of the Virginia State Capitol, 1779–1965." Master of Architectural History thesis, University of Virginia, 1981.

Lahendro, Joseph Dye. "Fiske Kimball: American Renaissance Historian." Master of Architectural History thesis, University of Virginia, 1982.

Latrobe, B. Henry. *The Correspondence and Miscellaneous Papers of Benjamin Henry Latrobe*. Edited by John C. Van Horne et al. 3 vols. *The Papers of Benjamin Henry Latrobe. Series 4, Correspondence and Miscellaneous Papers*. 3 vols. New Haven: Yale University Press for The Maryland Historical Society, 1984–1988.

———. *The Papers of Benjamin Henry Latrobe*. Microfiche edition. Edited by Thomas E. Jeffrey. Clifton, N.J.: James T. White and Co. for the Maryland Historical Society, 1976.

Lehmann, Karl. *Thomas Jefferson: American Humanist*. New York: Macmillan, 1947. Reprint, with a 1964 foreword by Dumas Malone. Charlottesville: University Press of Virginia, 1985.

Lybrock, Albert. Architectural Drawings and Plans, Virginia Capitol Building, 1858. Acc. 36480. General Architectural Files Collection, Library of Virginia.

McCormick, Thomas J. "Charles-Louis Clérisseau." *Papers of the American Association of Architectural Bibliographers* 4 (1967): 9–16.

———. *Charles-Louis Clérisseau and the Genesis of Neo-Classicism*. New York: Architectural History Foundation; Cambridge, Mass., and London, Eng.: MIT Press, 1990.

McRae, Sherwin. *Virginia State Capitol: An Historical Account of the Erection of the Capitol, and the Review of the Question of Its Preservation; Also a Brief Account of the Acquisition of the Public Square*. Richmond: N.p., 1871. First published in *Old Dominion Magazine* (15 Aug. 1871): 483–491.

McRoberts, Brian. "Reconstruction of Jefferson's Rotunda in the Virginia Capitol." *Classicist*, no. 2 (1995–1996): 76.

Malone, Dumas. *Jefferson and the Rights of Man*. Vol. 2 of *Jefferson and His Time*. 6 vols. Boston: Little, Brown and Company, 1948–1981.

Mordecai, Samuel. *Richmond in By-Gone Days: Being Reminiscences of an Old Citizen*. Richmond: Published by George M. West, 1856.

Nichols, Frederick Doveton, ed. *Thomas Jefferson's Architectural Drawings: Compiled and with Commentary and a Check List*. 4th ed. rev. and enl. Charlottesville: Thomas Jefferson Memorial Foundation and The University Press of Virginia, 1988. First published as *Thomas Jefferson's Architectural Drawings: A Massachusetts Historical Society Picture Book*. Foreword and descriptive notes by Frederick Doveton Nichols. Boston: Massachusetts Historical Society, 1960.

O'Neal, William Bainter. "An Intelligent Interest in Architecture: A Bibliography of Publications about Thomas Jefferson as an Architect, Together with an Iconography of the Nineteenth-Century Prints of the University of Virginia." *Papers of the American Association of Architectural Bibliographers* 6 (1969): 3–150.

————. *Jefferson's Fine Arts Library: His Selections for the University of Virginia Together with His Own Architectural Books*. Charlottesville: University Press of Virginia, 1976.

Palladio, Andrea. *I Quattro Libri dell'Architettura*. Venice: Dominico de' Franceschi, 1570.

————. *Les Quatre Livres de l'Architecture d'Andre Palladio*. Translated by Roland Fréart, sieur de Chambray. Paris: De l'Imprimerie d'Edme Martin, 1650.

————. *The Architecture of A. Palladio; In Four Books*. Edited by Giacomo Leoni. Translated by Nicholas Dubois. 4 vols. in 5. London: Printed by J[ohn] Watts, for the Author, 1715–1720; 2d ed. 2 vols. London: Printed by John Darby for the Author, 1721; 3d ed., corrected. 1 vol. With notes and remarks of Inigo Jones, an appendix containing *The Antiquities of Rome*, written by A. Palladio, and *A Discourse of the Fires of the Ancients*, never before translated. London: Printed for A. Ward, S. Birt, D. Browne, C. Davis, T. Osborne, and A. Millar, 1742.

————. *The Four Books of Andrea Palladio's Architecture*. Edited by Isaac Ware and translated by Ware and Richard Boyle, third earl of Burlington. 4 vols. in 1. London: I. Ware, 1738. Reprinted as Andrea Palladio, *The Four Books of Architecture*, with a new introduction by Adolf K. Placzek. New York: Dover Publications, 1965.

Peebles, John Kevan; Noland and Baskerville; Frye and Chesterman, Associated Architects. Architectural Drawings and Plans, Virginia State Capitol, 1904, 1904–1905, 1905. Acc. 36589. Drawings and Plans Collection, Library of Virginia.

Peterson, Merrill D., ed. *Thomas Jefferson: A Reference Biography*. New York: Charles Scribner's Sons, 1986.

Pevsner, Nikolaus. *A History of Building Types*. The A. W. Mellon Lectures in the Fine Arts at the National Gallery of Art, 1970. Bollingen Series 35, Vol. 19. Princeton, N.J.: Princeton University Press, 1976.

Poffenberger, Brien J. "Jefferson's Design of the Capitol of Virginia." Master of Architectural History thesis, University of Virginia, 1991.

Priddy, Sumpter T., III; and Martha C. Vick. "The Work of Clotworthy Stephenson, William Hodgson, and Henry Ingle in Richmond, Virginia, 1787–1806." *American Furniture* (1994): 206–233.

Prothro, Kimberly. "Thomas Jefferson's Virginia State Capitol: A Construction History, 1780s to 1854." Summer 1988. Virginia

State Capitol, Richmond, Va., Historic American Buildings Survey, HABS, VA, 44-KICA, 9-, American Memory, Historical Collections for the National Digital Library online database, Prints and Photographs Division, Library of Congress, Washington, D.C.

"Report of the Committee on the Enlargement, Restoration and Repair of the Capitol," 24 Jan. 1906, Doc. No. 3, *Journal of the Senate of . . . Virginia Begun . . . January 10, 1906*. Richmond: Davis Bottom, Superintendent of Public Printing, 1906.

"The Richmond Calamity." *Harper's Weekly* (14 May 1870): 313.

Richardson, Selden. "The Capitol Square That Never Was." *Virginia Cavalcade* 51 (winter 2001): 24–25.

Riddick. Susan C. "The Influence of B. H. Latrobe on Jefferson's Design for the University of Virginia." Master of Architectural History thesis, University of Virginia, 1988.

Roberts, George, and Mary Roberts. *Triumph on Fairmount: Fiske Kimball and the Philadelphia Museum of Art*. Philadelphia and New York: J. B. Lippincott, 1959.

Saadat, Ramin. "Jefferson, Palladio, Euhemerism, and the Virginia State Capitol." Master of Arts thesis, Virginia Commonwealth University, 1994.

Scott, Mary Wingfield, and Louise F. Catterall. *Virginia's Capitol Square: Its Building and Its Monuments*. Richmond: Valentine Museum, 1957.

Scott, W. W., and W. G. Stanard. *The Capitol of Virginia and of the Confederate States: Being a Descriptive and Historical Catalogue of the Public Square and Buildings, and of the Statuary, Paintings and Curios Therein*. Emendations by E. Griffith Dodson on the Library of Virginia's copy. Richmond: James E. Goode, Printer, 1894.

Sommer, Frank H., III. "Thomas Jefferson and the Reform of Virginia Architecture." Paper presented at "Classicism: Visions and Revisions, 1740–1990," Third Annual Symposium, Department of Architectural History, University of Virginia, Charlottesville, 1990.

———— "Thomas Jefferson's First Plan for a Virginia Building." In *Papers on American Art*. Edited by John C. Milley. Maple Shade, N.J.: Edinburgh Press for The Friends of Independence National Historical Park, 1976.

Sowerby, E. Millicent. *Catalogue of the Library of Thomas Jefferson*. 5 vols. Washington, D.C.: Library of Congress,

1952–1959. Reprint, Charlottesville: University Press of Virginia, 1983.

Specifications for Fire Proofing and Additions to the Virginia State Capitol, Richmond, Va., Capitol Enlargement Correspondence, Bills, and Receipts, 1902–1906. Virginia Governor (1902–1906: Montague), Executive Papers. Acc. 36710. State Government Records Collection, Library of Virginia.

Stillman, Damie. "From the Ancient Roman Republic to the New American One: Architecture for a New Nation." In *A Republic for the Ages: The United States Capitol and the Political Culture of the Early Republic*. Edited by Donald R. Kennon. Charlottesville and London: Published for the United States Capitol Historical Society by the University Press of Virginia, 1999.

Strother, Warren. "Restoring the Capitol: Behind Mr. Jefferson's 1785 Walls, an Interior for 1964." *Commonwealth* 30 (Feb. 1963): 21–25.

Szambien, Werner. *Le Musée d'Architecture*. Paris: Picard, 1988.

Treadway, Sandra Gioia, and Edward D. C. Campbell, Jr., eds. *The Common Wealth: Treasures from the Collections of the Library of Virginia*. Richmond: Library of Virginia, 1997.

Tyler-McGraw, Marie. *At the Falls: Richmond, Virginia, and Its People*. Chapel Hill: Published for the Valentine, the Museum of the Life and History of Richmond, by the University of North Carolina Press, 1994.

Virginia Division of the Budget. *The Virginia State Capitol, Richmond, Virginia*. Richmond: Division of the Budget, 1965.

Wallace, Charles M. *The History of the Capitol of Virginia: Being a Succinct Account of the Structure, with Notes on Many Striking Events Connected with It.* Richmond: Dietz Press, 1936.

Washington Statue and State Capitol Model, Records, 1786–1789, 1793, 1795–1796, 1802–1803. Auditor of Public Accounts, Inventory Entry No. 666, Library of Virginia.

Wenger, Mark R. "Jefferson's Designs for Remodeling the Governor's Palace." *Winterthur Portfolio* 32 (winter 1997): 223–242.

————. "Thomas Jefferson and the Virginia State Capitol." *Virginia Magazine of History and Biography* 101 (Jan. 1993): 77–102.

White, Joseph Senter, III. "Samuel Dobie, Thomas Jefferson, and the First Virginia Capitol in Richmond." Master of Arts thesis, Virginia Commonwealth University, 1997.

Wilson, Douglas L. "Dating Jefferson's Early Architectural Drawings." *Virginia Magazine of History and Biography* 101 (Jan. 1993): 53–76.

————. *Jefferson's Books*. Preface by Daniel J. Boorstin. Monticello Monograph Series. [Charlottesville]: Thomas Jefferson Memorial Foundation, 1996. Originally printed as "Jefferson's Library." In *Thomas Jefferson: A Reference Biography*. Edited by Merrill D. Peterson. New York: Charles Scribner's Sons, 1986.

Wootton, James E. "Jefferson's Capitol and Capitol Square: An Edifice of First Rate Dignity." *Virginia Cavalcade* 51 (winter 2001): 16–23.

Yorke, James. "Tiny Temples of Mr. Nash." *Country Life* 195 (8 Feb. 2001): 66–67.

Index

Page numbers in italics refer to illustrations.

The Capitol of Virginia: A Landmark of American Architecture was designed by Amy C. Winegardner, graphic designer at the Library of Virginia. Page layout was produced by Amy Wincgardner using Macintosh G4 and QuarkXpress 4.0. Text was composed in Granjon and Trade Gothic. Printed on acid-free Ultra Litho Satin, 80-lb. text by Sheridan Books, Inc., Chelsea, Michigan.